THE CHURCH'S DEBT TO HERETICS

THE CHURCH'S DEBT TO HERETICS

BY

RUFUS M. JONES

D.D., LITT.D., LL.D.

PROFESSOR OF PHILOSOPHY IN HAVERFORD COLLEGE, PENNSYLVANIA, U.S.A.,
AUTHOR OF "STUDIES IN MYSTICAL RELIGION," ETC.

SECOND IMPRESSION

WIPF & STOCK · Eugene, Oregon

Wipf and Stock Publishers
199 W 8th Ave, Suite 3
Eugene, OR 97401

The Church's Dept to Heretics
By Jones, Rufus M.
Copyright©1924 The Estate of Mary Hoxie Jones
ISBN 13: 978-1-59752-888-7
Publication date 4/1/2008
Previously published by James Clarke & Co., Limited, 192

PREFACE

My greatest difficulty in preparing this volume has been the problem of selection. There have been too many heretics for one small book ! The material vastly overflowed my limits of space. I was therefore compelled to choose a few specimens from the extensive prairie harvest which the centuries laid at my hand. Some readers no doubt will look in vain for their pet heretic, while others will perhaps find some one praised and glorified whom they would prefer to see burned or at least left to oblivion. I have, in any case, done my best in this brief space to be historically fair.

I owe very much indeed to my wife and to Emma Cadbury, Jun., who have helped me in the extensive reading and research that were necessary for the collection of facts, and I wish also to express my appreciation of the service which Dr. Henry J. Cadbury has rendered in reading the proof.

HAVERFORD COLLEGE,
    HAVERFORD, PENNSYLVANIA, U.S.A.
        December, 1924.

CONTENTS

CHAP.		PAGE
I.	WHO ARE THE HERETICS?	11
II.	THE GNOSTIC COMPLEX	28
III.	EARLY HERESIES ABOUT THE NATURE OF CHRIST	61
IV.	THE BATTLE WITH ARIANISM	85
V.	HERESIES OF THE HUMAN—"ALL TOO HUMAN"	104
VI.	HERESIES CONCERNING THE SPIRIT	131
VII.	THE BACKGROUND AND ENVIRONMENT OF ANTI-CHURCH HERESIES AND SCHISMS	162
VIII.	A HARVEST OF SECTS AND SCHISMS	184
IX.	HERETICAL MOVEMENTS IN THE REFORMATION PERIOD	216
X.	MODERN HERESIES AND HERETICS	243

THE CHURCH'S DEBT TO HERETICS

CHAPTER I

WHO ARE THE HERETICS?

It is manifestly impossible to discuss the contribution of heretics, or even to decide whether they have been destructive or constructive factors in the life of the Church, until we have first come to a carefully formed decision on the question, What is a heretic? We use the word so loosely in these modern times that the charge of heresy means little, while many persons even jauntily profess to be heretics and rejoice in wearing the badge. Once it was more dangerous to be thought a heretic than it was to be sent at the head of a besieging force to storm a castle; and nobody then, under any circumstances, ever admitted that he really *was* a heretic. The person who deviated from the larger group did so in the overwhelming conviction that he was right and the others were wrong. "If he stood alone in a howling wilderness he was more than a man; he was a church. He was the centre of the universe; it was round him that the stars swung. All the tortures torn out of forgotten hells could not make him admit that he was heretical."[1]

The heretics we are concerned with in this book will be, then, not these easy holiday heretics; they will be men and women who believed in their inmost souls that they had a heavenly vision, a divine revelation, of the way forward, and that it was given to them to be the bearers of the truth. They were ready for the uttermost sacrifice in behalf of the cause to which they were devoted. The capricious innovator, the freakish disturber, the hysterical champion of novelties, the unhappy rebel against whatever is, need not occupy us. We are interested here rather in discoveries of fresh insight, the recipients of new illumination, gifted leaders of unwon causes, prophets of neglected or forgotten truth, profound interpreters of the deeper significance of life.

But when does the term " heretic " rightly apply? When does a man cease to be counted safe and become a dangerous heretical adventurer? Not, of course, until certain truths have been accepted as sacred and have won a group of adherents who believe them to be both true and essential to life and salvation. There must be a conscious and intense orthodoxy in the field before there can be a standard that can be used to differentiate and determine heresy. Heresy is positive deviation within the

[1] G. K. Chesterton, *Heretics*, p. 11.

WHO ARE THE HERETICS?

fold from an established, or at least an accepted, set of doctrines or body of ideas. Doubt, scepticism, infidelity, are not heresy. They are indications of drift and uncertainty, and, perhaps, of the disintegration of faith, but they are too weak and negative to be called heresy. Heresy proclaims something to be true and important. It announces a way. It asserts a fiery positive. It has the emphasis of infallibility no less than orthodoxy has. The point of importance is that it challenges the ideas of orthodoxy and insists that something else is more true and closer to the eternal nature of things. Orthodoxy in all ages has been concerned with the preservation of an objective system that has come to be considered essential to salvation, since the mission of the Church, in the mind of the faithful, orthodox believer, is to be an instrument of salvation. Orthodoxy has thus, in the main, formed around the essentials for salvation and theories of eschatology. Heresies, on the other hand, have been more concerned with life, with experience, with maintaining a continuous revelation of the Spirit here and now. They have inclined to shift the emphasis from heaven to earth.

The word "heresy" itself in its early use means an *act of choice*, or a fixed *attachment*. The Catholic Church, when it was coming into being, called those persons "heretics" who followed *that which they had chosen for themselves*. In its later use "heresy" comes to mean a *sect*. It differs from schism in that the latter properly applies to ecclesiastical cleavage, not to faith and doctrine as does the former. In the strict sense we cannot rightly speak of heresy until the period is reached when the Church had come to be regarded as a divine institution, supernaturally equipped and endowed and ordained to be the depository and channel of truth and saving grace. As soon as the leaders of the Church began to emphasise the immense importance of sound doctrine it became necessary to have a sure criterion and standard of the faith, and quite naturally the Church came to occupy the position of guardian of what was believed to have been " once delivered " to its apostolic founders, and, as naturally, the Church was assumed to be possessed of an infallible capacity to keep the deposit of truth in its purity and wholeness. But long before this position became conscious and explicit, let us say by the time of Cyprian (died 258), in the middle of the third century, it had been an implicit attitude and a steadily growing tendency and practice. The fight with Gnosticism, which began a full century and more before Cyprian's day, forced the Church, as we shall see, to formulate its faith, and to search out the foundations of its authority. But there was a long formative period when authority was more or less subconscious and inarticulate, and when doctrine was being gestated and born, though it was not yet a fixed and unalterable body of truth.

If we go back a little farther, to the established system of Judaism—the Jewish *ecclesia* at Jerusalem

WHO ARE THE HERETICS?

—with its magnificent traditions, its immense antiquity, its claims to divine origin and equally divine authority, we shall be compelled to admit that Christ Himself and His apostolic followers, by the standards existing in their day, were " heretical." In fact, St. Paul accepted the challenge and used the very word " heresy " as applying to the way of life which he accepted : " I confess unto thee," he said to Felix, " that after the way which they call heresy, I serve the God of our fathers."[1] It was plainly enough Christ's deviation from the beaten track of orthodox teaching and prescribed practice which sent Him to the cross at the hands of the hierarchy. He boldly and unfavourably contrasted the moral regulations of the Mosaic code with His own teaching : " It hath been said, but I say." He so freely transformed the observance of the Sabbath day that His conception of the day was not their conception of it, and He fundamentally reinterpreted the existing conceptions of God, of man, of life, of purification, of holiness, of the Temple, of service, of sacrifice, of death and of the life beyond. The old wine skins could not hold His wine ; His gospel was new and unique, not a " patch " to be fitted to an ancestral garment. He was an innovator. He deviated decisively from the beaten path. He opened a new road—a different way of life and revelation—for men to go.

If by any chance Christ Himself had been taken

[1] Acts xxiv. 14.

THE CHURCH'S DEBT TO HERETICS

by His later followers as the model and pattern of the new way, and a serious attempt had been made to set up His life and teaching as the standard and norm for the Church, Christianity would have been something vastly different from what it became. Then "heresy" would have been, as it is not now, deviation from His way, His teaching, His spirit, His kingdom. Love and Life—not doctrine—would have been the sacred words, the spiritual realities for a Christian. Dedication to the work of bringing the kingdom of God, heroism, daring, adventure, self-giving, joy, radiance, abandon, readiness to go "the second mile," would have characterised Christians. What we may properly call "Galilean Christianity" had a short life, though there have been notable attempts to revive it and make it live again, and here and there spiritual prophets have insisted that anything else than this simple Galilean religion is "heresy"; but the main line of historic development has taken a different course and has marked the emphasis very differently. One trouble, too, with those attempts to return to the Galilean model has always been the tendency to copy some outward feature of Christ's life and teaching rather than to catch and reproduce the spirit of that life and teaching. The early Waldenses insisted on wearing sandals to be like Him. The Franciscans seized upon "poverty" as the sacred mark of relationship with Him. Thomas à Kempis was far too much under the spell of an ascetic Christ rather

WHO ARE THE HERETICS?

than that of the real Christ of the Gospels, though, notwithstanding that, his service to spiritual religion beyond all question is very great.

The actual character of the intellectual environment around the primitive Christian centres, humanly speaking, settled the line of development which Christian thought took, and quite naturally determined what was, as a consequence, to be considered heresy. Two great influences come into play from the earliest beginnings of the expansion of Christianity. The first converts to Christianity were either Jews or Greeks, and the influences from these two sources were paramount. The first group consisted of two classes, Palestinian Jews and Hellenistic Jews. The latter class lived in the Græco-Roman world and were possessed of a certain amount of Greek culture, and used the Greek language. The converts of the second order, whom I have called "Greeks," were often not of Greek stock and blood, but were peoples that had been Hellenised by the spread of Greek language and culture, though in the cities on the shores of the Ægean Sea, where a great part of St. Paul's missionary labours lay, the inhabitants were in large measure of ancient Greek stock. As is well known, it is impossible to do successful missionary work, to win men from an old religion to allegiance to a new one of a different type, without first adapting the message to the stock of ideas and the existing practices of those who are to be won. The transformations and the adjustments are usually

THE CHURCH'S DEBT TO HERETICS

made more or less unconsciously. They are not explicit compromises. In fact, the missionary may not be conscious that he has made any surrenders or that he has yielded any ground, but sooner or later the new converts will be found to have a different outlook, atmosphere, interpretation, slant of thought and tinge of feeling, as well as an altered set of reactions and practices, from those of the person who first proclaimed the message to them. The habits of thought and action of a people—what we call " the psychological climate," or " apperception mass "—together with their characteristic emotional tones, work powerfully, though silently, to alter and reshape whatever is transmitted. No truth can be passed on to a new race or to a people with its own peculiar habits of mind without entailing immense risk and peril. Some of the most vital features may be actually lost, while almost every aspect may be transformed. It will never be the " same " after it has been assimilated and interpreted through a new group of minds. Here, as in so many other ways,

> " Life, like a dome of many-coloured glass,
> Stains the white radiance of eternity."

The earliest transforming influence which wrought upon the Galilean way of life and thought was, of course, the Jewish body of ideas and practices in the midst of which it had come to birth, and especially the apocalyptic outlook and expectations with which many contemporary minds were saturated. It can-

WHO ARE THE HERETICS?

not yet be settled how far Christ Himself shared in apocalyptic hopes. There are two extreme positions, one of which makes Christ a teacher of the most intense apocalyptic and Messianic expectations; the other of which insists that His entire message was ethical and spiritual and wholly devoid of apocalyptic content. Both these extreme views are in pretty violent conflict respectively with large sections of the Gospel accounts, and neither of them seems likely to gain the final support of general expert judgment. But almost all scholars are now agreed that there was a steady growth of apocalyptic material in the period of the life of the Church during which the teaching of Christ was being brought into permanent literary form. Some of the later strata of the Gospels are more definitely apocalyptic in tone than are the earlier ones. The closer we press to the actual life and the very words themselves which He spoke, the less we find of material which relates Him to or links Him up with the popular hopes and expectations of the time, and the more He stands forth as a unique revelation of God's love and tenderness and as the Teacher of a moral and spiritual way of life, here and now, in this checker-board world of light and darkness, of life and death. The crassly materialistic expectations are almost certainly not His teaching. They are alien to Him and are taken over from the environment in which the living seed of His truth grew and developed. The fierce and destructive traits sometimes attri-

THE CHURCH'S DEBT TO HERETICS

buted to Him as Messiah do not belong to the original portrait of the gentle, radiant Galilean. There are many other tendencies, too, of Jewish thought and practice, tendencies toward a priestly system, memories of sacrificial rites, that have left their tint and colour on the new spiritual religion that was born amid ancient customs and habits, and that emerged only slowly into its own independent sphere of life and truth. The immense service of St. Paul in freeing the new from the yoke of bondage of the old can hardly be too strongly put, but even so the inheritance from the older Jewish stock remains a large and, in some respects, a heavy legacy, which would no doubt have been larger had not Jerusalem fallen in the year A.D. 70.

The influence of Greek life and thought is the greatest single factor in the profound transformation of Christianity from a way of life to an elaborate system of thought. Nobody who shared in effecting this great alteration of basis was consciously " heretical." It was a fact of " manifest destiny " ; the push of racial forces, a push which no man could have stemmed. The world of the first and second centuries was a confused and complex *mélange* of faiths, hopes, fears, philosophies, theosophies, mystic religions, and mysteries. If Christianity had insulated itself and had stood aloof from this " complex," it would have made no conquests, it would have recorded no triumphs. But, on the other hand, it could not " find " itself in and through that strange

WHO ARE THE HERETICS?

confluence of life and thought without at the same time "losing" itself as it had been in its purity, beauty and simplicity. The ancient Roman aqueduct was constructed on one single level. It went straight across country from its water source to the city it supplied, without regard to the contour of the earth and with no conformity to the slopes and bends of valley depressions. The waters of salvation cannot in like manner be piped straight through human history at a single level. They must follow the lines of life, and take the curvatures, the ups and downs, of this mixed human life that is to be watered. We must trust that, in the long run, these waters will rise once again to the height of their source and will go safely down the valleys and up again, as we have at length discovered that water by its nature will do.

The later chapters of this book will bring to light in detail the immense struggles and conflicts that were occasioned by the attempt to define and formulate the Christian faith in the thought-terms of the Græco-Roman world. I am only concerned now to point out that the main direction which the development of Christianity took was determined by the type of mind that was there waiting to be won over to its message and converted by its appeal, as the course of a river is determined by the contour of hills and valleys and by the slope and pitch of land. The Christian world has always been ready to recognise that the literature of the Old Testament was a large

THE CHURCH'S DEBT TO HERETICS

factor in the formation of the faith and doctrine of Christianity, and that body of literature has been taken over *in toto* as an integral part of our own Scriptures ; but that same Christian world has not to anything like an adequate degree recognised the immense influence of the Greek prophets : Heraclitus, Socrates, Plato, Aristotle, the Stoics and Plotinus, who, for better or worse, are indissolubly builded into the very structure of our Christian faith. They can no more be eliminated than can Abraham, Moses, David and Isaiah. Backgrounds of immemorial culture work in subtle fashion, and no councils, or infallible authorities, can successfully ban their influence. Our religion, then, even when we call it " orthodox," and approve it, is a vast mixture, a confluence of streams from many sources. It has come down not alone from Galilee and Judea ; it is not one simple stream " that flowed fast by the oracle of God." It has had ten thousand tributaries, and the contributions from foreign sources can no more be strained away than the Arve can be separated from the Rhone after they have once united their flood of waters at Geneva.

Fortunately we can make our way back even yet to the Headwaters of the mighty stream, and feel, if only dimly, the purity, the splendour, the beauty, the mystery and the power of the River of Life as it burst forth from the eternal depths. But when we come down to the lowlands, where it now runs in its wide, though shallower, bed, we find merged in

WHO ARE THE HERETICS?

one stream the indivisible waters from almost every land and people of the earth. We cannot recover the pure Galilean religion any more than we can recover Eden. Earthly paradises and pure perfections that have been in earlier, simpler ages cannot be " restored." We must go forward, not backward. The time-process is a one-way road. We must build our own faith, not inherit one from the past. For better or for worse we are living in the world of the twentieth century, and our lives must be lived amid the complexities which the cumulations of many generations have produced. We cannot bodily lift and take over for our spiritual uses the religious setting or the intellectual outlook of any former period. We can find inspiration, kindling power, leadership, eternal truth, immortal words, and the most dynamic Person of all the centuries when we go back to the Alpine heights where the stream began, but we must work out our own Church, our own faith, our own body of thought, our own interpretation, our own social order, and if we are ever to have a kingdom of God it must be the one we ourselves build by going forward with our faith and hope and love.

There is, then, no way of getting a fixed and static standard which settles outright and automatically what is heresy and who is a heretic. We all deviate from Christ. We all have wandered from the ways of life and thought which prevailed in the days of the apostolic Church. We cannot pick out

THE CHURCH'S DEBT TO HERETICS

texts of Holy Scripture and use them as quick and easy measuring instruments to determine the orthodoxy of men, though they do throw much illumination upon the paths in which we walk. If we are to use the word " heresy " with any exact meaning we must accept the testing standards which the historic Church itself has used. We must take as " heretics " those whom the Church has called heretics, those whom it has burned or banned. We must not, however, expect to find any universal and unchanging body of doctrine by which all future deviation is once for all settled. There can be found no infallible standard, held *semper et ubique et ab omnibus*, by which every individual, in every age and country, stands or falls. A heretic in one generation would have been a saint if he had lived in another, and a heretic in one country would often be a hero in another. We must be content to go to the conclusions of the dominant Church of the given period, and to pick out our heresies and our heretics from the indexes and the records of the time. If the Church decided that a given person was a heretic I shall admit him without further debate into the fellowship of those who have fought with minorities for unpopular truths, and who have suffered reproach and agony for daring to question what the authoritative majority approved. When I use the word " Church," I mean by it, first, the body of Christian believers in the days of the apostolic leaders. Then, next, I mean the historic Church,

WHO ARE THE HERETICS?

organised under authoritative Bishops, which eventually divided into the Eastern and Roman Catholic branches; and finally, I mean Protestant Christianity, with its denominations, communions and branches, called Churches, in so far as they act with authority toward those who deviate from the settled views and beliefs of the unyielding majority. Where the heresy "succeeds" in great enough measure the body which is called heretical by the mother Church may with some right itself be called by the same august name of Church, and may therewith henceforth proceed to have its own heretics. To succeed in constructing a conquering and permanently cumulative spiritual movement is, in the judgment of impartial history, to pass over to the safe side of that thin line which separates orthodoxy from heresy, though the original Church would be very slow to admit such a principle, for its doctrines seem to it to be infallibly and eternally true and "without reply," *i.e.*, not open to argument.

One further point needs a brief consideration, that is the question as to what is to be meant by the heretic's "contribution" to the life of the Church. There will be a great variation in the types of contribution. In some instances the Church has eventually—after the fight was ended—taken over nearly all the central ideas and practices of the specific heresy. I shall treat what is acquired through that method of slow absorption as a contribution, and I shall still call it a "contribution" even though the ideas so acquired may have proved later to be an unwise addition, which is undoubtedly the case with much that was absorbed from the Gnostics. In other instances heretics have mainly served the Church by awakening it from dullness and lethargy, and by stimulating it—" stinging " it, like a gadfly, as Socrates would say—to new life and power. They have driven it closer back upon the sources of its inner life and have thus brought it back from its wanderings to itself and its true mission. Again and again heretics have brought to light neglected or unemphasised truths. They have championed causes which, but for them, would have been " lost causes." They have made known the august authority of conscience and the immense value of the individual. They have borne a glorious testimony to the range and height of human daring and sacrifice, and they have given noble witness to the fact that one man with God on his side is unconquerable—if in fact God *is* on his side.

> " How think ye, the end ?
> Did I say ' without friend ' ?
> Say rather, from marge to blue marge
> The whole sky grew his targe
> With the sun's self for visible boss,
> While an Arm ran across
> Which the earth heaved beneath like a breast
> Where the wretch was safe prest !
> Do you see ? Just my vengeance complete,
> The man sprang to his feet,
> Stood erect, caught at God's skirts, and prayed !
> —So, *I* was afraid ! "

WHO ARE THE HERETICS?

The story will be a long, strange one, full of lights and shadows, tragedies and comedies, cruelty and tenderness, but it is a story of human life, and, on the whole, the telling of it will increase faith and heroism, and those realities by which men live.

CHAPTER II

THE GNOSTIC COMPLEX

THERE used to be a widespread theory that the first century of our era was a period of irreligion and indifference, in fact, of moral and spiritual collapse; that Christianity came to a world that had lost its faith and that was carefree and frivolous, without depth or seriousness. Almost exactly the opposite was the case. It was a time of great concern over the issues of life and death. Few centuries can be cited that have been more marked by a spirit of serious search for a way of salvation. To use Sir Gilbert Murray's phrase, the world of that era had " lost its nerve." There was a noticeable absence of peace, security and serenity. Men felt their lives enveloped in mystery, and in multitudinous ways dread powers of the universe disturbed and frightened them. They had no confidence in themselves, they felt no assurance that they were the masters of their fate or the captains of their soul. The old popular gods were outgrown and were thought of as weak and puerile, if they were thought of at all. But wherever one turns one finds an eager quest for divine light and help and guidance. Philo, Plutarch, Seneca and Epictetus are some of the most serious contemporary seekers

THE GNOSTIC COMPLEX

for truth, but the unnamed seekers were legion, and the common people, of the type who "heard Jesus gladly," were keen and earnest in every part of the vast Roman Empire.

Ever since Alexander the Great had "married the East and the West," and given the world a common language and culture there had been a steady interchange of ideas between East and West. The West had shown a strange fascination for the mysterious aspects of oriental religions, and there were periodic "invasions" of the West by the religions of the East. Especially keen was the Western appetite for "mystery religions," and for cults that offered a way of salvation for the individual soul. Christianity was only one of many religions which told men how they could be "saved." Everywhere it went it found rivals, but, in a very real sense, it came to a world that was waiting for it, and that was in some degree prepared for its message.

The New Testament itself furnishes some glimpses of the religious environment of primitive Christianity. The background is dimly sketched into the picture. We catch here and there intimations of rival movements and hints of cross-currents. It is plain enough that St. Paul did not speak or write to men on the shores of the Ægean whose minds were "empty, swept and garnished." They did not hear of "salvation" for the first time when they heard him preach, though the "way" which he preached did no doubt sound to them new and strange, as the

THE CHURCH'S DEBT TO HERETICS

Athenians noted. As soon as we look a little below the surface we find indications that there existed religious societies and associations almost everywhere ; societies, for instance, like the Essenes, or Orphic Circles, or Pythagorean brotherhoods, or mysteries of Mithras, or mysteries of Isis, or the devotees of " the Great Mother," all of whom believed that they were twice-born souls and were in possession of a way of genuine purification and of deliverance from this body of death. Besides these cults of salvation there were beginning to appear new types of esoteric societies, professing to find another way of salvation, salvation by discovery of " the great secret," revealed through magical knowledge, or Gnosis, which was set in contrast to " faith " that was assumed to be on a lower level.

There is a wide difference of opinion among scholars as to the date of the beginning of these movements and also as to the origin of them, but nobody who knows the facts doubts the importance of them, the extent and variety of the new faiths or the immense influence which they exerted. It is no exaggeration to say that by the middle of the second century the Church found itself engaged in a life and death struggle with the multitudinous forms of Gnostic religion. They did not by any means all use the word *Gnosis* (knowledge)—in fact, the word is seldom used—and they took different forms and modes of development, according to the personality of the leaders or according to the prevailing views

THE GNOSTIC COMPLEX

and conditions of special localities and periods ; but, with all their variations, they can quite well be grouped under the title which I have chosen, " The Gnostic Complex." In fact, " complex " seems a very appropriate word for these movements. The word properly means organised tendencies or sentiments which are in some degree confused, morbid and abnormal. They are usually found in individuals, but here in these movements we are confronted with social waves, or tides, or drifts, of morbid and unbalanced sentiments which were more or less " contagious." We have revealed to us in these movements a society which seems neurasthenic and psychopathic—suffering from nervous prostration—in which almost any " suggestion " may powerfully operate and effectively work.

A great many of the Gnostic societies are, of course, not rightly called heretical. They were often wholly outside the sphere and area of the Church. Some of them plainly antedate the birth of the Church, but they tended all the time to influence and colour its life and thought, and the movement was the fertile mother of heresies. Christianity has throughout all its history borne the marks of its conflict with this *mélange* of rival faiths, for while it was ostensibly victorious over them, it was at the same time in some degree " led captive " by those whom it conquered.

The Gnostic systems are not, in a proper sense of the word, forms of philosophy. They are, it is true,

THE CHURCH'S DEBT TO HERETICS

given to speculation about the origin of the world and the source of evil, but they were much more akin to magic than to philosophy, and they drew upon mythology and imagination for their constructive material rather than upon rational and verifiable grounds of truth. They were very skilful in their use of "the *débris* of ancient faiths," out of which they fashioned new and fantastic structures. They "plundered" the older faiths somewhat as the builders of new temples plundered the ancient shrines for their building material. The religions of Babylonia, Persia, Egypt, Asia Minor, the Old Testament and Greece, especially the imaginary world system set forth in Plato's *Timæus*, furnished suggestions, and sometimes even body and filling, for the weird Gnostic "gospel" during the prolific period of the first and second centuries.

The word "Gnosis," used in its technical and magical sense, first appears in 1 Tim. vi. 20, the writer of which is plainly living in an atmosphere charged with new and dangerous teaching—teaching which he calls "profane babblings" and then names *gnosis*, though he insists that this word, which usually means "knowledge," or "science," is falsely applied to this new brand of faith. The entire Epistle is concerned with this new and subtle danger which confronts the Church. "Old wives' fables," "profane and useless," he calls the rival doctrines. "The endless genealogies which minister questionings," mentioned in chap. i. 4, are quite obviously

THE GNOSTIC COMPLEX

to be found in Gnostic systems, while "the seducing spirits and doctrines of demons," "the hypocrisy of men that speak lies," "branded in their own conscience as with a hot iron" (chap. iv. 1–2), are just as certainly to be explained as references to these hated and dangerous opponents of the faith. When this Epistle and the other Pastorals, attributed to St. Paul, were written, the battle was on and the lines were sharply drawn. "The faith once delivered" is set over against the dangerous novelty, and we hear again and again of the "faithful saying which is worthy of acceptance by all," and which is intended to end the debate.

Ephesians and Colossians imply a somewhat different religious background, but they also clearly reveal the fact that the writer is shaping his message to offset a dangerous rival faith. He warns his readers of the danger of substituting "shadows" for *real things*, of being robbed of the prize of faith by adopting a form of "voluntary humility," "of worshipping angels" and of "intruding into those things which no man hath seen, vainly puffed up by the understanding of his fleshly mind" (Col. ii. 18). "Take heed," he writes, "lest there shall be any one that maketh spoil of you through his philosophy [speculation] and vain deceit, after the tradition of men, after the rudiments of the world" (Col. ii. 8). There is evidence in this Epistle and in Ephesians that a strongly ascetic movement is at this time disturbing the Christian Churches of Asia Minor, and that a " philosophy " is abroad which holds that the *flesh* is of undivine origin and intrinsically evil, as being composed of " matter." It appears further that some are taking up ascetic practices and humiliating ceremonies in the hope that they will thus be able to free themselves from the malevolent power of hostile angels or demons, what St. Paul calls " the world-rulers of this darkness, the spiritual hosts of wickedness in heavenly places," *i.e.*, in the sky (Eph. vi. 12). There must, too, be some specific significance in St. Paul's use of the Greek word $\pi\lambda\acute{\eta}\rho\omega\mu\alpha$ (pleroma), which is usually translated *fulness*. It occurs twice in the Epistle to the Colossians (i. 19 and ii. 9). Now this word *pleroma* holds a very important place in many of the Gnostic systems, where it has a technical meaning, as we shall see later. The word may have been in frequent use in the nascent sects of Asia Minor when this Epistle was written, or it may equally well be that the later Gnostics took the word over from St. Paul into their own systems, as they took over sacred words from the Fourth Gospel.[1]

Gnosticism in its explicit form was not yet on the stage, but the apostle is quite evidently confronted with a drift or wave of thought which belongs to the general " complex." It seems, furthermore, impossible not to admit that even in the earlier Epistles, especially in the Corinthian correspondence, St. Paul is aware of a widespread tendency to overvalue what

[1] See Abbé Duchesne's *Early Hist. of the Church*, Vol. I., p. 54, note.

THE GNOSTIC COMPLEX

he so often called *gnosis*, which is usually translated knowledge or wisdom, and which is contrasted sometimes with "love" and sometimes with "faith." St. Paul refers ironically on various occasions to *gnosis*, and he frequently contrasts sound, true knowledge with a false and boastful *gnosis*, which only puffs up the possessor of it. The little Epistle of Jude, where occurs the phrase, "the faith once for all delivered to the saints" (ver. 3), contains a reference to "those who make separations," and the immediate use of the word ψυχικός which means "psychical men," for those who do not have the spirit (pneuma), and thus are not "pneumatical men," indicates that he has some Gnostic sect in mind (ver. 19). They " set at nought dignities and blaspheme glories" (ver. 8). "They blaspheme whatever things they do not know" (ver. 10), by which is meant the Creator of the world and His creation. They are compared with Cain, Balaam and Korah (ver. 11). They are "clouds without water, carried along by the wind"; they are "autumn trees without fruit, twice dead and plucked up by the roots"; they are "wild waves of the sea, foaming out their own shame"; they are "wandering stars, for whom the blackness of darkness hath been reserved for ever" (vers. 12–13).

The "Nicolaitans," referred to in Revelation (chap. ii. 6, 15), formed, at the time when the Book was written, a developed and well-known sect. The author of Revelation has a horror of these sectaries similar to that which we have found expressed in Jude. They eat food offered to idols ; commit fornication ; they are likened to Balaam ; they " know the *deeps* of Satan." The Gnostics often used the word βάθος (bathos), *depth* or *deep*, as the ultimate source from which things have come forth. We find such expressions as the " deeps of God " and " the deeps of Satan," or again, " the deep things " or just " depth " ; they have a " prophetess " who is called " Jezebel," and they apparently have a secret, mysterious wisdom, or *gnosis*. This is all we know of them from the New Testament. From the early Church Fathers it is possible to supplement somewhat this meagre information. Irenæus (*c.* 137–202) describes the Nicolaitans as " a branch of the movement falsely called 'gnosis.' "[1] They are further referred to by Tertullian, Clement of Alexandria and Hippolytus. Clement's accounts are given in the *Stromata* (Books II. and III.), where the heretical movement is definitely linked up with Nicolaus, the proselyte of Antioch, who was appointed as a member of the Committee of Seven in Acts vi. 6.

Harnack, who has made an important study of the Nicolaitans,[2] concludes that they formed an organised sect which penetrated and disturbed the churches of Asia Minor and existed as late as A.D. 200. They were, he thinks, shamelessly immoral ; they taught

[1] *Against Heresies*, III. xi.
[2] See *Journal of Religion* (Chicago, July, 1923).

THE GNOSTIC COMPLEX

a dualism of good and evil, a divine and a satanic source ; they held a speculative theory of emanations in descending order from the Divine Fulness, these emanations being called " æons," as was the case in most Gnostic systems; they employed baptism in the name of Christ, and they insisted on faith in Him as an essential of " salvation." He thinks, further, that Nicolaus, one of the Seven, was a very rigorous ascetic ; that he separated from his wife as an act of ascetic renunciation, and that he laid down as his principle of life : " It is necessary to abuse the flesh," meaning by " abuse " to " maltreat " the body by the practice of strict asceticism, but that the sect which took his name interpreted the phrase in an opposite sense and made it a ground for loose and promiscuous living.[1]

There is one more Gnostic movement dimly and mysteriously in evidence in the New Testament, namely, the " Simonians," fathered by the famous Simon Magus of Acts viii. 9–24, who is called by all the early writers against heresies the founder of Gnostic theories.[2] He was called by the people of Samaria " the great power of God," and later, having faith and having accepted baptism, he tried to purchase the apostolic power.[3] His story is told with some detail in the romancing documents, the *Clementine Homilies* and *Recognitions*, and also in the *Acts of*

---
[1] Clement gives the account of Nicolaus' separation from his wife and his principle of action in *Strom.*, B. II.
[2] See especially Epiphanius, *Adv. Haer.*, XXI. and XXIV.
[3] Acts viii. 19.

THE CHURCH'S DEBT TO HERETICS

Peter and Paul, as well as in the writings of the early patristic heresy hunters. Simon appears as the founder of a sect. He claims to be a manifestation of " the Boundless Power of God." He was accompanied in his missionary travels by a woman who was called " Ennoia " (" the Thought of God ") and who was believed to be a reincarnation of Helen of Troy ! He held that the world is an emanation or series of evolutions from " the Boundless Power," through six stages, or " roots," or " æons," each emanation being a reflection of the one before and growing weaker and poorer as it becomes farther removed from " the Boundless Power," its ultimate source. Everything has a double aspect, male and female, and everything, again, is double in the sense that it is a union of *the good*, which comes from above, with " matter," which is from below and is always and everywhere *evil*.[1]

There is no overt mention of Cerinthus or of his sect in the New Testament, but there is an early tradition, which seems well founded, that he was an opponent of St. John in Ephesus, and it seems pretty certain that his heresy, or a similar one, is the background setting for the First Epistle of John. Irenæus, in his treatise *Against Heresies*, relates that he himself in his youth saw Polycarp who was " instructed in the faith by the Apostles and was personally

---

[1] For a more extended account of the " Simonians " the reader is referred to Legge's *Forerunners and Rivals of Christianity*, Vol. I., Chap. VI.

THE GNOSTIC COMPLEX

acquainted with many who had seen the Lord." He then proceeds to tell this incident: "Some heard him (Polycarp) say that John, the disciple of our Lord, went into the baths in Ephesus one day, but seeing Cerinthus inside, he rushed away from the baths without bathing, and said, ' Let us fly lest the baths fall, for Cerinthus, the foe of truth, is within.' "[1]

From the later patristic writers we can piece together the following story, though much of it is plainly built out of the stuff of imagination. Cerinthus was an Alexandrian Jew, strongly influenced by Philo. He produced a *blend* of religion which was a fusion of Judaism, Ebionitism, Oriental faiths and ideas and facts from Christianity. He devoted himself to the propagation of this strange blend, and set himself against Christian missionaries wherever he heard of their work. He is said to be "one of the circumcision" who contended with Peter (Acts xi. 2). He, again, is charged with being one of the "certain men who came down from Judæa and taught the brethren, saying, Except ye be circumcised after the custom of Moses ye cannot be saved" (Acts xv. 1). He gets the blame for being one of those who "troubled" the Gentile converts "with words subverting their souls" (Acts xv. 24). He is charged with being the "emissary" who disturbed the Galatian churches, and with being one of "the false brethren" referred to in Gal. ii. 4. Finally, he is

[1] *Op. cit.*, III., iii. 4.

supposed to be one of " the false apostles " and " deceitful workers " in 2 Cor. xi. 13.

Like Simon Magus, he seems to have been the formulator of a crude, primitive Gnosticism which furnished some of the lines on which the later systems were built. He believed in a single Supreme Being, far removed above the evil and chaos of this world, which was created by an inferior angelic power, perhaps by the same angel who " mediated " the law to Moses on Mount Sinai.

Jesus, he held, was born like any other man, of human parents—Joseph and Mary—but at His baptism the spiritual Christ, or the Holy Ghost, was sent by the Highest God to dwell in Him and to teach Him. As a result He was able to reveal the Unknown God, who is wholly unlike the Jehovah of the Old Testament. At the crucifixion Jesus alone suffered, while Christ withdrew and returned to heaven. Cerinthus also taught a fantastic millennial hope. There is a late tradition that John wrote his Gospel to refute Cerinthus and his disciples. A very much better case can be made to show that the first Epistle of John has his Christology in mind. " Who is a liar but he that denieth that Jesus is the Christ ? " may very well be aimed at Cerinthus. In any case it fits him perfectly. So, too, does a later passage, " Hereby know ye the Spirit of God : every spirit that confesseth that Jesus Christ is come in the flesh is of God : and every spirit that confesseth not Jesus is not of God : and this is the

THE GNOSTIC COMPLEX

spirit of the anti-Christ whereof ye have heard that it cometh ; and now *it is in the world already*" (1 John iv. 2–3).[1] This is certainly written to offset a Docetic theory of Christ, and the teaching of Cerinthus may well be the early stage of such a Docetism, as the Fathers indicate.

Here, then, are some glimpses into the background and margins which lay behind and around the Church in the period when the New Testament was being written.

Gnosticism was not yet developed into the strange, elaborate systems which were to become strong rivals of the Christian faith, but already at this early date there were drifts, waves, tendencies of thought abroad which contained the prolific seeds and germs of the later systems. Some of the most important of the sects formed in the second century were the Ophites, known also by many other names, especially " Naassenes," or " Naassendi," as they are often called by the early heresy reporters—Irenæus, Hippolytus and Epiphanius—the Valentinians, the followers of Bardesanes, and of Basilides. Still closer to the life of the Church than any of these, and more influential upon it, was the great separatist movement led by Marcion ; and finally, we must study the heresy of " Docetism," which was an abortive form of Christian faith that had, as we have seen, emerged even before the New Testament was finished.

---

[1] Some MSS. of the Epistle read " Every spirit that dissolveth or annulleth Jesus " (iv. 3a).

THE CHURCH'S DEBT TO HERETICS

This is not the place for a minute, detailed account of the particular Gnostic sects. They are decadent forms of religion, full of confusion, superstition, gullibility, credulity and wild imagination. It will be quite sufficient for the present purpose if I sketch briefly the main lines and the general characteristics of the movement as a whole. Gnosticism was not, as some scholars have tried to show, an attempt to " intellectualise," " rationalise," or " Hellenise " Christianity. It was an esoteric type of religion, which professed to have discovered a divine secret by a special revelation. This " revelation," which differed from sect to sect, was called "*gnosis*"— not properly " science " or " knowledge," but a mysterious " secret " which had been made known. Some of the sects, especially those that were semi-Christian, claimed that they possessed a secret tradition which had been communicated to their founders by Christ, and transmitted as a priceless tradition to them. Other sects claimed that their secret had been revealed to their founders through the sacred books of some ancient religion. The central concern of all Gnostic faiths was " salvation," which meant the deliverance of the soul, first from the contaminations of the material body, and secondly from " the powers of darkness " that were supposed to intervene between this world and the realm of light whither the soul is bound. This world is a dark and tragic arena, where contrary forces continually fight for us and against us. It is

THE GNOSTIC COMPLEX

a tangled skein of many opposing threads—a mixture of light and darkness, a dualism of spirit and matter.

The Gnostics relieved God of the responsibility for Creation. It is not His world. It is the bungling work of an apprentice, whom they call, after Plato, the demiurge, whose plan was inadequate, and whose stuff was abominably poor world-building material, namely "matter." All the systems of Gnosticism set forth a doctrine of emanations, or a reversed evolution from the Highest God, called the Pleroma, down through a series of beings thought of as living, creative, angelic forces, often called "æons," who are mediators of the Divine, the bringers of light. Only thus, by a system of descending beings, far removed from the Highest God, could they explain the actual condition of the world as an evil mixture and, at the same time, free Him of the onus and burden of making such a world. Somewhere in the descending spiritual chain was the demiurge, who took the refractory material stuff lying at his hand and made the best kind of work he could in the circumstances. Evil, then, is not to be charged against God. He has had nothing to do with it. He is absolutely good—only He is too far away to help us much and, just because of His purity and holiness, He cannot come into contact with matter and evil. The only hope of "salvation," therefore, lies in the possibility of having "relief expeditions" sent down to us, or in the communication of a "salvation-secret."

THE CHURCH'S DEBT TO HERETICS

Some Gnostics tell of one, and some of the other method. Some of them tell of a divine hero, who volunteered to come down here to enter into the tragedy with us, to join in the fight against darkness and evil and to bring redemption. The later systems, influenced by Christian teaching, introduce Christ among the " æons " as the Redeemer-Hero. Nearly all of them tell of a primal man, named variously Adam, Cadmon, or Gayomart, who was sometimes thought of as a divine being fallen, and sometimes as the redeeming-hero come to bring salvation. Many of the systems held that there are two, or even three types of men. The highest type is the man who is already redeemed. He is a pneumatical, or spiritual, man. Then there is the psychical, or natural, man, who can be redeemed by accepting Gnostic wisdom. Finally, there is the hylic, or material, man, who failed to have any spiritual qualities put into his being when he was made, and he is consequently forever " unsaveable " and non-elect. He is of the earth earthy.

The systems that were formed under Persian influences, directly or indirectly received, have much to say of the seven planetary spheres, called the Hebdomad. These spheres are ruled over by hostile angelic powers, whom St. Paul refers to as the " world-rulers of darkness," or " a spiritual host of wickedness in the heavenlies " (Eph. vi. 12). These hostile forces are supposed to have a certain power over our destiny here on earth, and to be able

THE GNOSTIC COMPLEX

to defeat the endeavours of the soul after death to reach the Ogdoad, or eighth realm, the realm of light and spirit, beyond the hostile Hebdomad. The Gnostic leaders claimed that they possessed the mysterious secret password by which the soul that knows it can get by the seven " keepers of gates " and attain the heavenly peace. It was this claim to a priceless secret—protection against evil spirits and the promise of life beyond the grave—which more than any other feature gave these confused movements their power of attraction and fascination over the men and women of the period.

The sect founded by Marcion was only in a limited sense part of the general Gnostic drift, but he was enough of a Gnostic to be quite properly treated in this chapter. He was by far the most important individual who came under the influence of Gnostic ideas, and he became the founder of a sect which was one of the most dangerous rivals the Church in all its history has ever had. Harnack considers him the most significant figure in Church history between St. Paul and St. Augustine, and he thinks that Catholicism was constructed mainly in opposition to Marcion, and that many of its foundation principles were learned from this major heretic.[1]

Marcion was born between A.D. 85 and 100, in Pontus, probably in the town of Sinope, which was the most important Greek commercial city on the

[1] A. Harnack, *Marcion : Das Evangelium vom fremden Gott* (Leipzig, 1921), Preface.

southern coast of the Black Sea. Tertullian opens his swelling attack on Marcion with many figurative references to the place of his birth : " Nothing in Pontus is so barbarous and sad as the fact that Marcion was born there, fouler than any Scythian, more roving than the waggon-life of the Sarmatian, more inhuman than the Massagete, more audacious than an Amazon, darker than the clouds of Pontus, colder than its winter, more brittle than its ice, more deceitful than the Ister, more craggy than Caucasus, more savage than the beasts of that barbarous region. What Pontic mouse ever had such gnawing powers as he who has gnawed the Gospels to pieces ? "[1]

Pontus had large communities, and from very early times there were large and flourishing Christian churches in the general region, and in Sinope in particular. Hippolytus says that Marcion's father was Bishop of Sinope, and there is no reason to doubt it. In fact, it is quite within the range of possibility that Marcion himself may have been ordained at some period of his life. He was a shipmaster of Pontus, and he travelled widely. It is impossible to tell when he first began to deviate from the prevailing line of Christian thought, or at what age he emerged as a propagandist. Irenæus relates a savage reception given to Marcion once by Polycarp, which was probably in Asia Minor, in the early period of his heretical activity. At their meeting Marcion said to Polycarp, " Do you

[1] *Against Marcion*, I. i.

THE GNOSTIC COMPLEX

recognise me?" "Yes," answered Polycarp, "I recognise you as the first-born of Satan." It would seem from the heat of the good man that Marcion already must have had a notorious reputation for heresy.

He went to Rome, according to tradition, in his own ship, very early in the reign of Antoninus Pius, and joined the Roman Church, giving it a present of 200,000 sesterces (which would be about £1,400, or $7,000).[1] Here, in Rome, he set himself to the task of carefully working out the foundations of his teaching in his great critical work, the *Antitheses*, which consisted of passages about the nature of God taken from the Old Testament and put side by side with passages from the sayings of Jesus and from the writings of St. Paul. He also prepared a text of the Gospel and a canon of St. Paul's Epistles. He appears to have brought his literary work to completion about the year A.D. 144, which is probably the year of his break with the Roman Church. The Church rejected Marcion's doctrine, returned the 200,000 sesterces to him and excommunicated him as a heretic. Undaunted by the catastrophe, he threw himself with tremendous energy into the work of propaganda and organisation, and in a few years launched a system which rivalled the august Church itself. Justin, writing about A.D. 150, while Marcion was still alive, says in his *First Apology*: "There is Marcion, a man of Pontus, who is even at this day

[1] Told by Tertullian, *Presc. of Her.*, XXX.

alive, and teaching his disciples to believe in some other god greater than the Creator. And he, by the aid of the devils, has caused many of *every nation* to speak blasphemies and to deny that God is the maker of this universe."[1]

Tertullian is still more emphatic, implying a danger that Marcion's heretical tradition *may fill the whole world*.[2] The date and manner of his death are uncertain. We only know that he left behind a powerfully organised rival church which lived for three hundred years in the West, and survived even much longer in the East, where it was finally absorbed into the Manichæan sects of the time. Here, then, is a heretic of large and serious proportions.[3]

Marcion's point of departure from the orthodox tradition is to be found in his interpretation of St. Paul, who, for him, is the one true apostle of Christ. He starts with the Pauline opposition between " law " and " gospel," that is, between a stern, malevolent justice on the one hand, and a tender, merciful love on the other. The Galatian and Roman Epistles influenced Marcion even more profoundly than they did Luther thirteen hundred years later. The former found in them his whole theory of the Old and New Testaments and his entire basic conception of creation and salvation. " The law," as it appears in St. Paul, represents, according to Marcion,

[1] *Op. cit.*, XXVI.
[2] Tert., *Against Marc.*, V. 19.
[3] In the account which follows, I am greatly indebted to Harnack's monograph, already referred to.

THE GNOSTIC COMPLEX

a wholly different god from the God whom Christ revealed. The Old Testament god is the creator of the world. He is *just*, but without mercy. His world, like his law, is full of darkness and thunder. It is a scene of tragic drama, unrelieved by love or forgiveness. The most comforting words of the Old Testament are really only illusion. Even the chosen people and the elect race are marched off into exile when they offend their jealous god. Suddenly, without any preparation for the event, the Good God, who up to that moment was unknown and unrevealed, sent His Son to the world to reveal Himself and to redeem men from the reign of the god of creation and law. But the world was foreign territory. He was a stranger in it. The world and its god, the law and its scribes, all set themselves against this new Revealer and Redeemer. He could not use the forces of the world—they were not His forces. He was alone, an alien here, unprotected, with no defences and no helpers. He was killed by the servants of the old god, who knew Him not nor comprehended His mission. But, in spite of all this, Christ succeeded. He revealed, even in His death, the new God, the stranger God, the loving and forgiving God—His Father.

For the first time the realm of the god of the Old Testament—the god of creation and law—was invaded by the God of goodness, and He now set Himself to the work of redeeming those whom the hostile god had made prisoners in his evil world and had kept in bondage and slavery to his hard, stern "law." The Gospel is thus wholly *new*, and salvation means deliverance from the power and sway of the lower god, the god of the Old Testament. This is the Gnostic tincture in Marcion's system. He does not have a speculative system of "æons" like the Gnostics, but he has instead, two Gods, one who has created a world full of evil and who has kept men in bondage in it, and the other " a Stranger God," a Divine Lover, who has invaded it to save as many as He can from the tragic scene. Marcion with this theory in his mind quite naturally became the sworn foe of the Old Testament and all its works. He believed that he was the true successor of St. Paul. The latter, he thinks, gave his life in the fight against the " law " and its defenders. Paul, he holds, is the one true representative of the Gospel, which he was determined to free from the trammels of the " law " and from the machinations of " the Judaisers " who were loyal to the god of the Old Testament. Peter and the other disciples never understood who Christ really was. They were always playing a pitiful *rôle*, for they were always entrenched in the old system and so could not be true and loyal to the new. They are " the false apostles " of Galatians and Second Corinthians. St. Paul alone was called directly by Christ and by God the Father to be an apostle and to deliver the Gospel from its enemies and its many corruptions.

By some mysterious process of interpretation

THE GNOSTIC COMPLEX

Marcion came to the conclusion that St. Paul recognised only one authentic written Gospel—the one divine communication which Christ left behind to convey His message. By a train of thought which we cannot now altogether trace, he decided upon St. Luke's Gospel as the true one, though even that had, he believed, been "doctored" by the "false apostles and the Judaisers," who also made additions to St. Paul's Epistles.[1] Marcion felt that it was his mission to " restore " this Gospel and St. Paul's Epistles to their pristine purity. The following are the twelve standard principles which formed the basis for his corrections and omissions, with which he made the Gospel and Epistles fit :

1. The creator and god of the Old Testament cannot be the Father of Jesus Christ. The former is "just" and unkind ; his promises are for the Jewish people, and are earthly.
2. The Old Testament cannot have foretold what was fulfilled in Christ ; it cannot be cited by Christ or Paul as an authority. Law and prophets are only to be understood literally, *i.e.*, they are not to be treated as allegory.
3. The good God must have been unknown to the world creator until after His appearance.
4. He cannot be represented as the director of the world, much less as the God of earthly providence.
5. He cannot appear as a judge, but only as the merciful Father and the Redeemer.
6. His redemption and His promises refer exclusively to eternal life.
7. The Son of the Stranger God, Christ, is to be regarded as a mode in His relation to the Father.

---

[1] Marcion probably chose St. Luke's Gospel because it was more strongly ascetic than the others, and because it may very likely have been the first to reach Pontus and to be used in the Churches of that region.

THE CHURCH'S DEBT TO HERETICS

8. He had nothing earthly about Him; hence no flesh, no body. He cannot have been born or had relatives.[1]

9. He did not fulfil the law, but annulled it; revealed the decided contrast between law and gospel, and based His redemption only on faith.

10. He asks from men complete separation from the world and the works of the world creator.

11. He called only *one* true Apostle after the original ones proved themselves unteachable; the gospel of Paul is the gospel of Christ.

12. He will not reappear as judge, but at the end of the days will declare the great separation which has been completed.[2]

In the Marcionite church we have distinctly the religion of a book—the book being composed of the Gospel and Epistles, interpreted by the *Antitheses*. He rejected mysteries, secret wisdom, special inspirations or revelations and philosophy. He bowed in wonder and amazement before the written story of a marvellous revelation and a no less marvellous redemption. He finds an absolute break between the old and the new, between the god whom he hated and God whom he adored, between the terror of the law and the grace of Christ. He is one of the greatest ascetics in religious history, and naturally so. He reckons the world and all that belongs to it to be the work of the god whom he hates. Propagation of offspring receives his bitterest denunciation. The whole method of it fits the creator-god, who provided for it. The flesh which this creator made is a factory of filth, a bubbling mass of coarseness and nastiness. He would admit no one to baptism in

[1] By this principle Marcion shows his strong Docetic bent.
[2] See Harnack, *op. cit.*, pp. 60–61.

THE GNOSTIC COMPLEX

his church who was living in the state of marriage. Hostility to the world, to the flesh, to human civilisation, could hardly go farther than Marcion went, and yet the men and women of his time flocked to him in shoals and risked life and all that was dear to join his rival church !

As we have seen, especially in the eighth principle of his scripture canon, Marcion was an extreme advocate of Docetism, which, in his period, was a widely prevalent view, both outside the Christian Church and within its area. It was thus a common Gnostic position, and it was, at the same time, a taking heresy, a very contagious idea. It was not so much an organised " system " of thought, fathered by some arch-heretic, as it was a tendency, a " drift." It was probably the earliest *overt* heresy to appear in the life of the Church, and, as has been pointed out, it was already an ominous symptom when the later books of the New Testament were being written.

Docetism really means a doctrine of phantasm, or a theory of illusion or seeming. The Docetists denied the *reality* of Christ's human nature—they are evidently not all dead ! Some, as Marcion, for example, denied it altogether ; others denied the fact of His human birth, His sufferings, and, of course, His death. They admitted that eyewitnesses *saw* Him with a body ; saw Him *seem* to suffer and to die, but they held that all this was illusion, or " seeming," as when one sees the oar bent in the water. That is the reason for the name, as the word

THE CHURCH'S DEBT TO HERETICS

" Docetists " means " Illusionists." The attitude, the theory, is a natural outgrowth of Gnosticism, a corollary of it. God can have nothing to do with matter ; the Divine cannot conceivably be brought into contact with material flesh, least of all, be incarnated in it. It is another of those interesting cases where logic comes into sharp collision with experience, and the Docetic elects to accept and to follow *logic*. My late friend, A. Clutton-Brock, was absolutely right when he said, " There is only one fatal heresy about Christ, namely, the heresy called Docetic, which robs Him of all reality." [1] All other heresies but this one are forgivable. To reduce Christ to a phantasm, so that He can be fitted neatly into a theory of matter, is to miss the blazoned track of life altogether. And yet how often, in one form or another, it has been done ! Few tendencies have been more common than the tendency to weaken the hold upon Christ's humanity, and to make Him seem *unreal*, foreign to our life and our world—a visitant here and not a genuine partaker in our life, our struggles, our problems, our sufferings.

Some of the Docetists—Cerdo, for example, who is said by some of the Fathers to have been Marcion's teacher—held that Christ " appeared " suddenly in the world, without birth, without being born as a man is born ; others held that Christ came *through* the Virgin. Still others held that Jesus was born as a man and remained in all essentials a man until His

[1] *Studies in Christianity*, p. 72.

THE GNOSTIC COMPLEX

baptism, when Christ descended upon Him from heaven and manifested Himself through the human Jesus, but left Him and returned to heaven, either before the passion or at the moment of the death on the cross. That view is probably referred to in 1 John v. 5–6 : " Who is He that overcometh the world but He that believeth that Jesus is the Son of God ? This is He that came by water and blood, even Jesus Christ ; not with the water only, but with the water and with the blood," *i.e.*, He was present not only at the baptism, but as well when His blood flowed out on the cross.

Other theories maintained that in the crowd on the way to Golgotha Simon of Cyrene was substituted for Christ and that he was crucified in Christ's stead, while Christ Himself, in the form of Simon, watched the event and then escaped. These crude makeshifts, however, do not properly rank with " pure " Docetism. They are bungling and evasive ways of getting around the material facts. The strict Docetist frankly admits that Christ *seemed* to be born, to eat, to drink, to grow weary, to suffer, to weep, to carry His cross, and to die in agony, but that it was all an illusion, like a vast cinematograph show, as we should say to-day, made to look like real events. A large amount of *tendency* literature was produced by the Docetists to set forth their doctrine. Imaginative books were written and floated with the pseudonyms of great personalities to catch the unwary. The *Gospel of Peter* is one of these interesting literary ventures. It says, describing the crucifixion : " He held His peace as in no wise having pain." And then again at the end, when, according to this Gospel, Christ left Jesus and was taken up, Jesus cried : " My power, My power, hast thou forsaken me ? " The *Acts of Peter*, with its story of *Quo vadis, domine*, and also the *Gospel of Thomas* and the *Acts of Thomas*, are of Gnostic origin and show this Docetic tendency.

Polycarp in his *Epistle to the Philippians* is strongly exercised over the contamination of this heresy—and he uses these strong words : " Whosoever does not confess the testimony of the cross [*i.e.*, that Christ suffered] is of the devil." Ignatius, too, the noble Bishop of Antioch and the heroic martyr in the Coliseum, was more distressed over the threatening dangers of Docetism than he was over his approaching contest with lions in the arena. Almost every one of his seven Epistles refers to the peril of this heresy. The passage about it in the Epistle to the Trallians is one of the most touching references : " If as some that are without God, that is the unbelieving, say, His suffering was only a semblance (but it is they who are merely a semblance), then for what reason am I now in bonds and ready to fight the wild beasts ? In such a case I die in vain and am guilty of falsehood to the cross of the Lord."[1]

Such, then, was the first great assault on the nature of Christ. It did not strike primarily against

[1] *Op. cit.*, Chap. X.

THE GNOSTIC COMPLEX

His divinity, it struck against His humanity. It came very early in the infancy of the Church. Irenæus says that Simon Magus, who was a contemporary of Jesus and was already a Gnostic teacher when the Church was born, taught that the Redeemer had " appeared among men as a man, though He was not a man, and was thought to have suffered in Judea, though He did not suffer."[1] It had to be met, along with the still more powerful drift of thought out of which it emerged, even before the Church was well out of its swaddling clothes. One of the most striking effects of the struggle on the Church itself was the great impulse which it gave towards its consolidation. It drew the loyal membership together into a more intense unity. It aroused it to produce a solid, integrated organisation and an authoritative hierarchy. One sees this at its strongest in the impassioned Epistles of Ignatius who was about to die. The struggle with Gnosticism and Docetism greatly hastened the formation of a definite canon of Scripture. Marcion's truncated canon awakened the Church to its need of a complete canon which should be the final criterion in a controversy about facts. It further impressed the importance of having a standard confession and rule of faith. The Apostles' Creed bears a most powerful testimony to the intensity of this struggle. The backbone of this creed was formed in the days when the contest was still intense and it is plainly enough

[1] Irenæus, *Against Her.*, I. xxiii. Simon himself is the " Redeemer."

THE CHURCH'S DEBT TO HERETICS

"a battle-creed." Almost every sentence bears the marks of the fight. " I believe in God the Father Almighty, Maker of heaven and earth," attacks the whole conception of æons and demiurges and asserts that *God Himself is the creator*. " I believe in Jesus Christ, His only Son our Lord, who was conceived by the Holy Ghost, born of the Virgin Mary, suffered under Pontius Pilate, was crucified, dead and buried," strikes at the entire welter of Docetic suppositions and imaginations and affirms the *reality* of the human events.

The list of subtle influences which crept into the Church and into the minds of believers from the Gnostic environment of the times is a long and important one, and in many cases the incoming " contributions " cannot be counted as assets. The thought of God as distant, remote and absentee was partly the result of this situation, and so, too, was the growing emphasis put on intermediary beings, from seraphim to angels. The belief in invisible hostile powers, already in evidence in St. Paul's later Epistles, became an ever greater factor as the Catholic system took shape. The dualism of good and evil, of light and darkness, of spirit and matter, of the world " yonder " and this world, which was so pronounced a feature of the Gnostic systems, came little by little to be a settled attitude also within the Church itself, and with this dualistic outlook came by a natural course an asceticism like that which prevailed in the Gnostic groups. It was, of course,

THE GNOSTIC COMPLEX

not alone the Gnostic tendencies which carried Christian believers into this world-hating, flesh-hating, self-hating state of mind. It was a part of the mental habit of the age. It was almost as difficult to escape it as to escape the pressure of the air. But Gnosticism was obsessed with the idea of the evil tincture of matter, and the Gnostic movements brought that idea to a new intensity and contributed strongly to its contagious quality. It was as though Buddhism had dropped some of its traits, and then had habilitated itself in western clothes. However completely Gnosticism itself might be conquered and ended as a live movement, this ascetic habit of mind which sprang from it, this world-fleeing spirit, could not be eradicated. The importance of sacraments was decidedly heightened, and the idea of their *meaning* transformed by contact with the Gnostic movements. These movements had laid a peculiar stress upon the miraculous and magic character of sacraments, which were supposed to have been mysteriously initiated and mysteriously communicated to those who possessed the divine Gnostic secret. They were in most groups thought to be essential for safety in the soul's fight with invisible forces, and equally indispensable for final salvation. It is easy to see, in the glowing pages of Ignatius, how this magic and mysterious character of the Christian sacraments possesses his mind, in a way entirely different from what appears in the mind of any New Testament writer. Ignatius, already in the first quarter of the second century, regarded the sacrament of the Lord's supper as "the medicine of immortality,"[1] and the supernaturally endowed bishop had become in his mind an indispensable requisite of a Christian church.

Here, then, in this conflict with Gnosticism, we may see the Church face to face with strong currents of thought which threatened to overwhelm it almost as soon as it was born. It came into being in a world that had its own opinions about salvation, and its own theories about the universe. These opinions, these theories, these "complexes," as I have called them, could not be ignored, nor could they be conquered by a method of annihilation. In fact, they were "conquered" by a gradual, and for the most part unconscious, process of absorption. There have been, and still are, persistent, age-long features of Christianity which are due not to the central Alpine stream of life that came forth from Christ, but rather to flatter, more shallow tributaries which ran in from the currents of thought that had their sources in primitive religions, and in bizarre mythical explanations of the problems of life and death, of light and darkness, of good and evil.

[1] Ignatius, *To the Eph.*, XX.

CHAPTER III

EARLY HERESIES ABOUT THE NATURE OF CHRIST

IT was inevitable that men should try to solve the mystery of Christ's nature. As soon as it became a central faith of the Church that Christ *saves* men, the question of His ultimate nature at once became an urgent matter. Everybody at this stage of thought admitted that only a divine being could impart salvation, but it was not easy to settle what was to be meant by "divine being." The Greeks were familiar with demi-gods and semi-divine heroes. Some of them were supposed to come down among men from the divine world, and some of them were human beings divinely exalted. But these mythological fancies belonged to the stage of polytheism. Such childish ideas did not fit the Jewish faith in one only God. How could there, then, be two divine beings? God certainly could not be thought of as divided. It was, too, according to their ways of thinking, just as impossible for any human being to *become* divine. The Divine is forever an indivisible One, and the human forever belongs down here in this undivine world. There seemed, therefore, no way to bridge the chasm. Here was a challenging problem of the most baffling sort. It had to be solved, for salvation was at stake upon it, and yet it seemed logically insoluble. It emerged in the first century, and it became the paramount question for three hundred years—and it still is for many a very live issue.

Dr. A. C. McGiffert, in his *God of the Early Christians*, has very well pointed out that the Christians of the early period had a great variety of views about God, largely determined, of course, by their previous training and environment. Gentile Christians, of the unphilosophical type usually, he thinks, thought of Jesus Christ as the only divine being they needed. They had found salvation through Him. He had first filled life with meaning for them, and they simply and naïvely took Him as Lord of their lives. If it had not been for the Jewish Christians, with their matured conception of God, the Creator of the world and the Ruler of history, and for the philosophers with their intellectual views of an eternal spiritual principle, this early, simple, Christian idea would long have prevailed, and would have satisfied the minds of the rank and file. But the deeper questions could not be kept down. The philosophers and question-askers were busy, and would not allow the simple members to be content with a Saviour-Christ whose origin was unexplained.

It is doubtful whether there has ever been a more creative work of genius than that which built, by slow and gradual processes of mind and faith, the

HERESIES ABOUT NATURE OF CHRIST

conception of God which came to be accepted as true and orthodox. The experience and the philosophy of all lands and all centuries are built into it, and, of course, it was not forged without vast controversies and disagreements, and in this work the so-called heretics played a great *rôle*. In fact, the final orthodox faith would never have been built without these same heretics. The early Apologists —Justin Martyr, Aristides, Minucius Felix, Tatian, Irenæus and Tertullian—were the first Christian teachers to begin the formulation of a definite doctrine, though St. Paul and the writer of the Johannine books had already been laying the foundations for the later builders. The Apologists were at one with their predecessor Philo, the Jew of Alexandria, and with the contemporary thinkers in the schools of philosophy in holding that God is self-existent, unchangeable, eternal, and, of course, above and beyond everything mutable and finite. They took it for granted that they could not know Him as He is in His own essential being, because, in their view, He does not possess qualities, or distinctions, or characteristics, as objects of our experience do. He could be known to men only through revelations of Himself, but these revelations at best, they held, are of necessity only manifestations, lower and secondary expressions of Him—not He Himself. He remains forever hidden and unseen— the Revealer of the revelations, the Manifestor *behind* the manifestations.

THE CHURCH'S DEBT TO HERETICS

The supreme revelation of God they called the *Logos*. It is almost impossible to translate this Greek word, for there is no one word which renders its meaning. It had already had a long history, both among the Greek and the Hebrew thinkers, and both strands of thought are woven together in the Christian use of the famous word. Heraclitus of Ephesus first used it five hundred years before Christ, and the Stoics took it over from him. Heraclitus represents a mystical reaction against the materialism of the early philosophers of Miletus. He declares that amidst the flux and mutability of things there is an intelligent Power that steers all affairs and events of the world, and he calls this Power the Logos. For the later Stoics, the Logos was thought of as divine Reason immanent in the universe, a rational Soul vitalising and guiding all that is. The Jews who wrote "the Wisdom Literature" introduced the term, "Wisdom of God," which they thought of as personified and as creative. It was a very short step to identify "the Wisdom of God," and what had earlier been meant among the Hebrews by "the Word of God," with the Greek Logos. Philo, the famous Hellenist, in the first half of the first century, fused the Greek and the Hebrew conceptions into one single *blend* of immense importance and of momentous future influence. For him the Logos becomes the sacred name for all of God that can be revealed or manifested. The Logos is God's

HERESIES ABOUT NATURE OF CHRIST

expression, His utterance of Himself, His Word. Logos is wisdom, intelligence, mind, thought, will-purpose. Logos stands for God in all His outgoing, creative, revealing activities. He is the divine Agent, the Image of God, the first-born Son of God, sometimes called by Philo and by later writers *deuteros theos*—" the second God."

In the early use of the word, Logos meant God—God thought of as intelligence, rationality and purpose. This was true also in Stoic circles. The Logos was the ultimate intelligent Reality of the universe. But as the tendency toward dualism increased, and God came to be thought of as an Absolute one, withdrawn from all contact with the world and with change and process, it became a necessity of thought to have some intermediary between God and the world. The Gnostics, as we have seen, bridged the chasm with a chain of subordinate beings. The Logos came to be thought of in many circles, especially in anti-Gnostic circles, as the connecting and mediating link between God and the visible universe.

The fourth Gospel, in its opening words, had already identified Christ with the Logos, who was with God and was God, and the Apologists and their successors followed boldly its great suggestion. All the ideas and activities which had clustered around the Logos were now attributed to Christ. He was pre-existent before His incarnation, as St. Paul had already assumed. He is the divine Agent, the active Reason, the operative Power of God. He is sprung from, or begotten by God, and yet is an absolute unity with God. He is personalised as Christ and yet in all His activities He is identical with God. He creates; He reveals; He mediates between the infinite and the finite. He is first-born and only Son; He is "second God," *i.e.*, *God as He is revealed*.

Tertullian goes considerably farther than the early Apologists did, though he is simply carrying their conceptions on toward their logical development. Creation for him is an essential part of the revelation of God, and, as against the Gnostics, Tertullian holds that it was the work of Christ, the Logos, "by whom the worlds were made." He makes the differentiation of the Logos from God more sharp and definite than the earlier writers had done, insisting, as he does, on the use of the Latin word *persona* both for God and for the Logos. Origen (186–253) was much more profoundly philosophical than any of the earlier interpreters had been, and he worked out the Logos doctrine more systematically than any of his predecessors had done. God is thought of as an absolute unity beyond and above all difference, forever the exact opposite of the mutable and the manifold. But though constant and immutable in His own being, He *eternally begets* the Son, the creative Logos who is the consciousness and the activity of God—God in procession and revelation. This Logos-doctrine is, then, the first

HERESIES ABOUT NATURE OF CHRIST

great speculative stage of Christian thought. It is an outstanding instance of the way in which Christianity seizes upon current, prevailing conceptions in the world of thought, and utilises them in the interpretation of its central truths. Logos-speculation was hoary with age when the great Christian thinkers laid hold of it and used it as though it had been an inherent feature of Christ's own message about Himself. It soon became a part of the necessary air which learned Christians breathed, a settled doctrine and a natural habit of thought. But it was not altogether a happy acquisition. It compelled thinking Christians to concentrate upon speculation. It was destined eventually to carry later thinkers much farther than the earlier ones had intended to go. There was, as there so often is, an irresistible maturing of the original idea, and its implications proved to be very complex and elaborate. It quite naturally, too, put Christianity at the mercy—never, alas! too tender—of logicians and intellectual speculators, and it carried along with it a separation between scholars and lay-Christians, logic-men and plain disciples.

The Logos-doctrine was no sooner formulated and raised to its high place in the speculative systems of Christian theology than the unorganised forces of Christianity began to attack it and to start the long series of movements which eventually dislodged it. Some thought that it tended too much to identify Christ with the creation, to link Him up with the visible world. Others were opposed to it because it was too abstract and speculative, too far removed from the simplicity of the Gospels. It seemed to some to be too much like the Gnostic systems, with a mysterious Logos substituted for the chain of æons. In any case, a vague and shadowy Being, far removed from human contacts, was taking the place of the tender and friendly Person who had come to show men the Father.

The first specific revolt against this elaborate doctrine was carried on by a small group of heretics who were given the appropriate nickname of " Alogi," *i.e.*, " those who oppose the Logos." Unfortunately there is extremely little known about the movement or about its leaders. Epiphanius says that Hippolytus described them in his lost treatise, the *Syntagma*.[1] But we are here too far away from primary sources of information to feel much assurance about what is reported as the teaching or the motives of these so-called " deniers of the Logos." It is quite probable that they were opposing the identification of Christ with the Logos as it is used in the Prologue of the Fourth Gospel, rather than the later and more elaborate Logos-doctrines, since the " Alogi " appear to have rejected this Gospel.[2] In any case we are warranted in assuming that there was, under this name, an early movement of protest against putting a mysterious metaphysical Logos in

[1] Epiphanius, *Haer.*, LI.
[2] See Harnack, *Hist. of Dog.*, Vol. III., p. 15.

HERESIES ABOUT NATURE OF CHRIST

the place of the Christ of the synoptic Gospels. There appear to have been many simple-minded Christian believers throughout the second century, as well as in the first, who were evangelicals in the early sense. They wanted to guard and preserve the *Evangel*, the good news about God and man and the kingdom, and they were not willing to see this precious and beautiful primitive message wrecked by elaborate metaphysical arguments. The main difficulty was that when they set themselves to counteract the dominant tendency to " exalt " Christ into a supernatural Visitor from another world, they themselves tended by a necessity of the case to " reduce " Him to human proportions and to end with a *this-world* being.

A much more important movement, and one marked by many divergent branches, was that which the early opponents of heresy called " Monarchianism." The term first appears in Tertullian, though he uses it as though it were already familiar. It was used to designate a conception of God which maintained His *absolute oneness* (monos). The nature of Christ and of the Holy Spirit must therefore be conceived in such a way that their existence in no way imperils the indivisible unity of God. There is only *one* Being who in substance and essence can be called God. Tertullian, in a well-known passage says : " So it is either the Father *or* the Son, and the day is not the same as the night ; nor is the Father the same as the Son, in such a way that both of them should be one, and one or the other should be both—an opinion which the most conceited Monarchians maintain."[1] The Monarchians recognised the danger, which always threatened Christian theologians, of falling into the pagan habit of admitting a plurality of divine beings. It was a fatally easy step for the converts from any of the religions in the Roman Empire, except only the Jewish. These uncompromising Christian monotheists therefore resolved to risk everything else to preserve and safeguard the faith in one God. What they risked was the essentially divine nature of Christ.

The earliest form of Monarchian doctrine was the humanitarian view of " the Adoptionists," who were so named from the fact that they held Christ to have been a man whom God *adopted* to be His Son. At first they were called Theodotians from one Theodotus, who gave the early formulation of this humanitarian idea. He was a leather dealer of Byzantium who came to Rome, probably during the papacy of Victor (190–200 A.D.). Hippolytus says of him : " Having taken his idea of Christ from the school of the Gnostics and from Cerinthus and Ebion, he considers that He (Christ) appeared in some such fashion as this : Jesus was a man begotten from a virgin according to the Father's will, living the common life of man. And having become most pious, He at length, on His baptism in the Jordan,

[1] Tertullian, *Against Praxeas*, Chap. X.

HERESIES ABOUT NATURE OF CHRIST

received the Christ from on high, who descended in the form of a dove. Wherefore the powers within Him did not become active until the Spirit which came down was manifest in Him, which Spirit declared Him to be Christ. But some will have it that He did not become God on the descent of the Spirit, and others that this took place on the resurrection from the dead."[1]

The followers of Theodotus appear to have collected and emphasised passages of Scripture which favoured their position while they were blind to the passages that conflicted with their view. In this selective manner they endeavoured to prove Christ to have been a man until the moment of His divine adoption. They were hostile to the spiritualising method of interpreting Scripture—the popular method of allegory—and set themselves to work to produce a sounder and more scientific method of interpretation, based upon a careful, critical study of grammar and rhetoric. Their leader was excommunicated sometime before the year 199 A.D. on the charge that he held "the God-denying apostasy that Christ was mere man," and they attempted without much success to form a church of their own. Eusebius gives an interesting glimpse of their scientific temper of mind. He says, quoting from a work

[1] Hippolytus, *Philosophumena*, VII., 23. Hippolytus here makes the blunder of tracing the sect of the Ebionites to Ebion, a heretic assumed to be somewhat like Cerinthus. There was no such heretic founder. The name "Ebionite" means "the Poor." Robert Browning made the same mistake in his poem, *A Death in the Desert*, where he says: "This Ebion, this Cerinthus or their mates."

THE CHURCH'S DEBT TO HERETICS

called *Little Labyrinth* : " They have falsified the holy Scriptures without scruple, rejected the standards of the ancient faith, and do not know Christ. They do not examine what the Scriptures say, but carefully strive after what logical syllogisms they could obtain from it that would prove their godless teaching. If anyone brings before them a passage from Holy Scripture, they ask whether a conjunctive or disjunctive syllogism can be made of it. They set aside the holy Scriptures of God, and employ themselves, instead, with geometry, being men who are earthly and talk of what is earthly and know not him who comes from above "—and much more to the same effect.[1]

A second Theodotus, a banker, or "moneychanger," as Hippolytus calls him, was a disciple and follower of the former Theodotus. He introduced the mysterious figure of Melchizedek, and claimed that there had been manifestations of Christ before He descended upon Jesus. The greatest of these was the manifestation through Melchizedek, the King of Peace and Righteousness, who was born " without father or mother," while Jesus was the Son of Mary. Artemon was another exponent of the Adoptionist view, and he is served up in the *Little Labyrinth* as one of the heretics of this group who refused to call Jesus Christ " God." The movement was loose and more or less unorganised.

---

[1] Eusebius, *Church History*, Book V., chap. 28. The writer is hardly giving an unprejudiced report.

HERESIES ABOUT NATURE OF CHRIST

It was for a long period a widespread *tendency* of thought to assume that Jesus was a man and was raised to the height of a divine being by an act of adoption, and by a bestowal upon Him of the Christ-Spirit or of the Holy Spirit.

The humanising, or anti-logos, tendency found one of its ablest and most famous exponents in Paul of Samosata. He was a native of Samosata, at that time the royal city of Syria. He became a friend of the far-famed Zenobia, Queen of Palmyra, and a prominent salaried officer under her patronage. He was a contemporary, and quite possibly a friend, of Longinus, the distinguished scholar and rhetorician, who lived in Antioch of Syria. Paul rose to the dignity of bishop and, at the time of his deposition, probably in the year 269, he was Patriarch of Antioch. The great Alexandrian Christians were engaged in the work of forging out the systematic theology which was in time to give final shape to the orthodox position. Antioch, on the other hand, was ambitious to have the intellectual leadership of the Church and to be independent of the Alexandrian school and its thinkers. It was a centre of culture and of liberality. It belonged at this period not to the Roman Empire but to the kingdom of Palmyra under Queen Zenobia, and Paul's troubles were due as much to political entanglements as to theological complications. The Roman faction consistently opposed him and the Zenobia faction strenuously favoured him.

THE CHURCH'S DEBT TO HERETICS

Paul was resolved, at all hazards, to maintain the humanity of Jesus. He insisted that He was born a man, grew up as a man and was as a man baptised by John. But He was anointed by the Spirit, given divine grace and power in a unique degree, and the eternal Logos, or pre-existent Wisdom of God, came to dwell in Him as a resident dwells in a house. This Logos is not thought of by Paul as a separate Person. He is rather the Wisdom, the creative Power, the revealing Aspect, of God. As a living Presence He operated upon and energised in Jesus until the latter became *one* in love and spirit with God. His mind and disposition were brought into perfect harmony with God. The unity of will was so complete that Jesus triumphed over temptation and made a full conquest of sin, living a sinless life. Jesus thus, through this indwelling Presence, became in a real sense the revelation and manifestation of God. Paul, however, would admit nothing that supported the doctrine of two deities. God must be thought of as for ever the One and Only God. He eliminated from his edition of the Psalms every implication which seemed to attribute essential divinity to Christ, that is, everything that implied that He was a "second God."

Paul's supreme interest was life, not metaphysics. It was to glorify character and experience, not logic. "What is given by nature," he says, "is devoid of merit." He wants a Christ who has attained and achieved His divine love and grace, not one who

HERESIES ABOUT NATURE OF CHRIST

was *made perfect* from all eternity. Divinity for him was a mark of character, of love and spiritual power, not a matter of *origin*. He is concerned with a God who is living, loving and personal, not an abstraction of metaphysics, and he is concerned with a Christ who lives and loves and learns, and has a real history and biography. Christ *becomes* one with God by harmony of will and unity of love.

Three synods were held to deal with Paul's teaching. The first two failed to condemn him, as he was under the powerful protection of Zenobia, but as the Queen's influence waned and the political power of the Roman party increased, a condemnation was secured and Paul was excommunicated, though he continued to exercise his functions as bishop until Antioch was taken by the Emperor Aurelian in 272.[1] In a letter signed by the Bishop of Jerusalem and five other Eastern bishops condemning Paul as a heretic, they declare that they have a settled authoritative standard—" the faith which we received from the beginning and possess, it having been transmitted and kept in the Catholic Church, proclaimed up to our day by the successors of the blessed apostles, who were eye-witnesses and ministers of the Word." Already in their minds the basis of orthodoxy was authoritatively settled and the essential Divine nature of Christ was a necessary part of it.

The next stage of heresy is generally called

[1] The history of these three Synods is given in Hefele's *Hist. of Church Councils*, translated by W. R. Clark (Edin., 1871), Vol. I., pp. 118-126.

THE CHURCH'S DEBT TO HERETICS

Modalism. It is a new form of Monarchianism. It aims to save the unity of God. Those who took the Modalist position held that there is one God, the ultimate Source, the Alpha of all manifestation, but being behind or above all that appears, He is, and must for ever remain, in His essence unknown and unknowable. We men can only know *a manifested God*. We can know a God only who comes forth and shows Himself in energies, attributes, or *modes*. This abstract, unknown God behind the scene does not concern us or interest us. Our business, as human beings, with souls to save, the Modalist holds, is with the revealed God who has made Himself known.

Noetus, a native of Smyrna, is one of the early exponents of Modalism. He definitely identified God and Christ, that is, Christ is God revealed, expressed, manifested. The unknown God has in Christ become known. The God who concerns us is the God whom men have seen in Christ. The identification is made so complete by Noetus that his opponents and critics called him a " Patripassian." If Christ is God, then, the opponents say, that means that the Father suffered, was crucified on the cross. Tertullian, in his treatise, *Against Praxeas*, is the first to apply the opprobrious label. The " Patripassians" replied by calling their opponents " Ditheists," *i.e.*, believers in two gods. They themselves were determined to guard the unity of God, and to maintain the full, uncompromised deity of Christ. It

HERESIES ABOUT NATURE OF CHRIST

was, no doubt, a bold and daring proclamation to say that Christ was God, but these " heretics " were honestly trying to glorify God and to hold fast to a faith in a divine Christ. Noetus was expelled from the Church in Smyrna, and thereupon he set up a school to propagate his views. Later he went to Rome, where he found views similar to his own being taught. They had been started by Praxeas, whom Tertullian attacked as a " Patripassian." Pope Zephyrinus was inclined to accept a Modalist view, and Noetus made friends and disciples in Rome. He found many texts of Scripture that favoured his position and, as is usual with theologians, he failed to see those that militated against it. He skilfully parried the charge of making God suffer by saying that the immutable and impassible God could not suffer in His essential nature, but He put Himself into visibility in Christ and only as Son He suffered, which made Tertullian call the Modalist god " a turncoat god." Some of the disciples of this doctrine, however, were ready to take the logical consequences of their daring position. Cleomenes, who was one of them, absolutely identified Father and Son, and admitted that God was nailed to the cross and was pierced with the lance, and was in every sense a suffering God. It was to meet such a view as this that one of the early creeds—that of Aquileia—began with the words : " I believe in God the Father, omnipotent, invisible and impassible."

There is in one of the churches of Italy a picture

of the crucifixion which shows the nails going through the hands of Christ, and through the beams of the cross into the hands of God the Father, who is dimly seen behind the cross. It is crude enough, both in idea and in design, but it is nearer the truth than is the ancient creed of Aquileia. We shall not return to Noetus, or to the Patripassians of Zephyrinus' age; but somehow, logically or alogically, we must hold fast to the faith that God suffers with us, and that our sins do pierce, if not His hands, His tender Spirit.

The great fight against Modalism, however, centres around Sabellius, whose name came to be almost synonymous with "heresy," and peculiarly with the heresy of "Monarchianism." Sabellius has no history, no biography. His antecedents are almost as untraceable as are those of the shadowy Melchizedek. He was perhaps from Libya—a native of Pentapolis—for Basil, the Cappadocian, calls him "the Libyan," and his views, in any case, were widely held in Egypt; but he had a long career in Rome in the papacy of Callistus (217-222), and it is not inconceivable that he was born in Rome. His writings are scant and doubtful. Hippolytus, his fierce opponent, is the main source for his opinions. Pope Callistus excommunicated Sabellius in 220, but Hippolytus claims that the Pope acted from fear of being charged with the same heresy himself, and that, in fact, he was all the time a "Sabellian."[1]

[1] *Philosophumena*, B. IX., 2.

HERESIES ABOUT NATURE OF CHRIST

Sabellius probably began as a disciple of Noetus, but he advanced and developed the Modalist doctrine to its logical fulfilment. He found a place, as the earlier Modalists had not done, for the Holy Spirit. In fact, he is the real founder of the doctrine of what is called "the economic Trinity," which means the Trinity revealed to man, as distinguished from "an essential Trinity." God, he insists, is absolutely one indivisible substance, but with three fundamental activities. He has appeared in temporal history under three successive aspects: as Father, who created the world and gave the Mosaic law; as Son, who came to be world-Redeemer; as Holy Spirit, the invisible divine Presence with men. These three modes of God are like the three modes under which light manifests itself to us. We may know it, first, as pure, white radiance, or, secondly, we may know it as the spectral colour band, such as we see it in the rainbow, or, finally, we may know it as actinic energy, the energy which transforms the sensitive camera plate, or which operates on the leaves of a tree or plant, producing chlorophyll. No one manifestation exhausts, *i.e.*, completely expresses, the infinite fulness of the divine Being, but He has shown Himself to the world in these three modes, the Father, the Son, and the Spirit, somewhat as our own life shows itself as body, soul, and spirit. Sabellius used the Greek word πρόσωπον for each one of the three successive modes of God. This word was in general use for the part played by an actor on the theatre stage. It did not mean "person" in the full sense, but rather *dramatis persona*, a "presented personality," a dramatic *rôle*, and in the end it was rejected by the orthodox as an inadequate word for the three members of the Trinity.

The Modalism of Sabellius was not orthodoxy; it was considered to be heresy, but it was a positive step toward the final orthodoxy of Nicæa. It formulated a full-fledged doctrine of the Trinity. It brought fresh suggestions as to the infinite richness of the divine Nature. As soon as the transition was made from " the economic Trinity " to the eternal and essential Trinity, which was the forward step, the orthodox position was achieved. Before the Council of Nicæa the lines of definition were vague and " fringy." Neither heretics nor orthodox believers were on sure ground. They all found it well-nigh impossible to guard at the same time both the unity of God and the humanity of Christ. When they came out strongly for one of these aspects of the truth, they generally lost the other aspect. The heretics, in the main, were less profoundly metaphysical than were the orthodox theologians. The former took the Gospel story more simply and naïvely than did the latter, and they did not trouble to think out all the implications of their honest and straightforward expositions of Christian faith.

Between these vaguer, tentative theories of Christ's nature, and the final orthodox view which emerged

HERESIES ABOUT NATURE OF CHRIST

from the struggle with Arianism, stands the great thinker—a colossal figure—Origen (185-253). He came to his manhood during the years when Christianity was engaged in a very stubborn battle with Paganism and with the Roman Empire. His father, Leonidas, was martyred when Origen was only a youth, and he himself also courted martyrdom. He had in a high degree the temper and spirit of a martyr. Six of his early converts died that death, but he, though showing unlimited daring and taking many risks, escaped, or, as he would have put it, "missed," the martyr's crown.

Few men have ever lived who possessed greater intellectual powers, greater depth and breadth of intellect, and at the same time his was a mind fused with a unique and wonderful spiritual fervour and consecration. He was a student in the famous Catechetical School of Alexandria under both Pantaenus and Clement, and he was himself informally made head of this School at the age of eighteen, the older teachers having been driven away by the furious persecution under Severus. At a later time he attended the lectures of the pagan philosopher, Ammonius Saccas, where he was fellow-student with Plotinus. He made a thorough study of Plato and of Numenius, and was in all his thinking profoundly influenced by the contemporary Neo-Platonic movement. He understood his age and spoke its intellectual language. Harnack is probably right in saying that Origen did more than any other man to win the Old World to the Christian religion. His life was full of stress and storm, with controversies surging around him, but, in spite of this, he produced an immense amount of sound, creative work, an amount perhaps unsurpassed by any other Christian scholar who has ever lived. The last twenty years of his life were passed at Cæsarea, in Palestine, where, during the Decian persecution, he was tortured on the rack, bound with chains and an iron collar in prison and threatened with the stake. This imprisonment lasted for two years, when, on the death of Decius in 251, Origen was liberated. He was, however, broken in body and did not long survive, dying probably in 253.

God, Origen taught, is a perfect Unity, a self-existent Being, indivisible, incorporeal, unchangeable, above and beyond space and time, pure Mind, *i.e.*, without anything that corresponds to emotions or passions. Christ, the Son, or Logos, of God, has expressed in His incarnation all of the divine Nature that can be expressed in the limitations of space and time. This Logos never at any time *began* to be. He is *eternally begotten* by the Father, as light is always emitted by a luminous body. God could not *be* God if He did not have a Son. In the incarnation the eternal Logos was united with an absolutely pure and sinless soul, and with a body equally pure and perfect, so that God's real Nature radiated and shone through Him unhindered. He was "the God-Man." Origen is not always clear

HERESIES ABOUT NATURE OF CHRIST

and consistent in his teaching about the Holy Spirit, though he is an unwavering Trinitarian of the "essential" type, and he always thinks of the Holy Spirit as co-equal and co-eternal with the Father and the Son. Origen seems, therefore, to belong to the far right wing among the extreme orthodox, and it would be very rash certainly to claim him as a heretic, but the historical fact remains that the heretics of the next generation constantly appealed for support to his writings, and both sides in a number of later controversies found ground for their positions in his books. The real basis which Origen gave to the later heretics for their claim of support in his writings was his tendency to make Christ *subordinate* to the Father, for they built strongly upon this point of subordination. Origen held that Christ is θεός ; God is ὁ θεός. The first means divinity ; the second essential deity. In any case, his profound and voluminous work *settled* none of the prevailing theological issues. It was possible to interpret him in more than one way. One could always ask : " What, precisely, did Origen *mean ?* " And so the storm raged around him as well as around the previous issues !

Theological discussion and speculation became from this time forward almost a disease. Gregory of Nyssa has given a humorous picture of these doctrinal discussions at a somewhat later time, but it fits this period as well : " Every corner and nook of the city is full of men who discuss incomprehensible

THE CHURCH'S DEBT TO HERETICS

subjects ; the streets, the markets ; the people who sell old clothes ; those who sit at the tables of money-changers ; those who deal in provisions. Ask a man how many oboli a thing comes to, he gives you a specimen of dogmatising on generated or ungenerated being. Inquire the price of bread, you are answered, ' The Father is greater than the Son, and the Son is subordinate to the Father.' Ask if your bath is ready, and you are answered, ' The Son of God was created out of nothing ! ' "

The time was ripe for a theological *crisis*, and it broke suddenly upon the world with a mighty, shattering force. We shall study that " crisis " in the next chapter. The point to note and to mark is this : The lines were all the time being formed during these struggles for the decisive issue. The material was being gathered for a final formulation, and every individual in the previous groups and every movement which is here reviewed made some contributions to the growing faith of the Church.

CHAPTER IV

THE BATTLE WITH ARIANISM

IT is somewhat difficult for a person who has a practical mind and who is eager to see the actual reign of God advanced to have any patience with the Arian battle, which seems to him a futile struggle over dim abstractions. Fourth-century Christians seem to such a person to be fighting in the thin air, having slight contact with reality and seldom touching *terra firma*. It ought, however, to be always interesting to see what men in any generation care for most, and it surely is important to discover how the central Christian doctrines have been formed; " in what a forge and what a heat " the great faith of the ages was wrought out. Creeds do not drop from the sky ready made. They are always deeply scarred with the marks of earthly battles, and for the most part the issue is worth the fight; the truth is usually clarified and advanced by the conflict. In one sense it was a single individual who tore open the chasm; in another sense it was the irresistible push of a great unsolved problem which would not " down " until the issue was really *settled*. Arius was the single individual, and the unsolved problem was the true nature of Christ.

THE CHURCH'S DEBT TO HERETICS

Arius was a highly gifted man who fascinated his hearers and aroused a loyalty to him that was almost fanatical. He was tall and gaunt, his hair tangled, his eye piercing, his movements quick and nervous. He was a musical genius, and he hit upon the idea of popularising his doctrines by composing hymns set to the tunes of the banquet halls of the time. He was strongly ascetic in his way of life, strict, rigid, pure, and though very attractive to the ladies and " going about from house to house," he yet lived an unimpeachable life, free from all scandal. He was logical-minded in his mental processes ; dry, cold, clear, but somewhat thin in his intellectual range. He was an African by birth, but he studied in Antioch rather than in Alexandria, and in the famous school of the former city he came under the influence of Lucian, the real founder of that school. Lucian is called by Harnack the real originator of the heresy, " the Arius before Arius." He had been a disciple of Paul of Samosata, but later he came under the influence of Origen, and finally produced a " blend " of the doctrines of these two men. He was revered by his scholars, and he laid his mind and spirit upon them. He suffered martyrdom about 311, and this tended to raise him still higher in the love and admiration of his disciples, among whom was Eusebius of Nicomedia, the most influential bishop of the Arian wing.

Arius returned to Alexandria, was ordained a deacon, and later was made a presbyter and became

THE BATTLE WITH ARIANISM

pastor over the church of Baucalis, not far from Alexandria. He was now in a theological atmosphere very different from that of Antioch, and being of a contentious disposition, he easily became a centre of controversy. He began the trouble himself by launching a charge of heresy—Sabellianism—against Alexander, the Bishop of Alexandria. The bishop retaliated by accusing Arius in turn of not being sound, and so the battle, which lasted over three hundred years, began. Arius, in his early period, took the position that Christ had been *made*, or *created by God out of non-existence*, *i.e.*, out of nothing, and it followed logically, of course, that there was a time when He was not, or, to omit the troublesome word *time*, "Once He was not." He began to be, and being made, or created, by the Father, Christ must necessarily be subordinate to Him who made Him.

Arius was condemned and excommunicated in 321 by Alexander in a synod of nearly one hundred African bishops. He fled to Palestine and there laid the plans for his campaign. He wrote a statement of his position to Eusebius of Nicomedia, a favourite of Constantine, and he received strong encouragement from Eusebius, to whom he soon went. While in Nicomedia, which was the imperial capital, he wrote in both prose and verse a popular defence of his position in a book called *Thalia*. This contained catching songs, so that his views came to be sung in the streets by the masses, who cared nothing for the deeper issues involved.

THE CHURCH'S DEBT TO HERETICS

As far as his position can be constructed out of the fragments that have come down to us, and from the statements of orthodox opponents and the early historians, Arius held very positively the unity of God, the one eternal, essential and indivisible, divine Being. He can have no equal, no other—He is God alone. Arius staked his whole case upon the preservation of the uniqueness of God. He was strongly Aristotelian in his intellectual position.[1] God, for Arius, is transcendent. He is yonder, not here. He remains for ever in Himself and to Himself and by Himself. He cannot be revealed. Arius would have endorsed the famous inscription in the temple of Isis : " I am he that was, and is, and ever shall be, and my veil hath no one lifted." His line, therefore, between Father and Son, was bound to be sharply drawn. He was logically compelled to make his conception of Christ fit in at whatever cost with this Monarchian God.

Christ must be another being than God. He is, in fact, a *created* being, though the first to be created. God, being one and indivisible, could not *beget* a Son out of Himself. God could and did create, before the worlds were made, an independent being of exalted wisdom and power, who was the instrument of creation. This is the Logos, the Son, the Christ, but He is separate from God and substantially different. He belongs in every sense to

---

[1] Orthodoxy was in the main Platonic in its general direction, while heresy drew inspiration from Aristotle.

THE BATTLE WITH ARIANISM

the world of created things. At the incarnation Christ took on a body, but He did not have a human soul, as the Logos took the place in Him of the soul, so that in real fact Christ was neither God nor man. He was lower than God and higher than man, but He could reveal the nature of neither. God remains an unknown God. By free act of will and by holiness of life Christ raised Himself to the full height of a Son of God. He achieved Sonship, and so, Arius held, though not God, He is worthy of worship and of divine honours.

Arianism is thus very simple and direct, clear-cut, easy to interpret and sharply marked off from orthodoxy. It is often called " Unitarianism," but it is characteristically different from the historical forms of Unitarianism. Christ is not a good man—He is not a man at all. He is a third being, intermediary between God and man, but He is to be worshipped as a divine being, something like a pagan demi-god, only greater. In fact Arianism was not properly a Christian faith; it was essentially pagan philosophy, and poor philosophy at that, though Arius endeavoured to build his teaching around certain well-selected texts of Scripture which gave it the chrism and odour of sanctity.

Under normal conditions this crude mixture of Christianity and pagan philosophy would not have been a serious menace to the Church; it would have been but a passing cloud across the sky. But it corresponded and tallied with a very peculiar world

THE CHURCH'S DEBT TO HERETICS

situation which made it a dangerous leaven. Christianity was just emerging as the recognised and established religion of the Empire. Constantine had made it a lawful religion by the Edict of Milan in 312. In 323 he became sole Emperor, and henceforth positively identified himself with the Christian religion, though, like many others of that period, he deferred his baptism. Multitudes of men and women were at this time flocking to the Church ; entire regions of the empire accepted Christianity in a day. They had, however, quite naturally only a thin veneer of the religion which they so easily adopted under the potent influence of the Emperor. They brought in their old divinities with them as new Christian saints ; their old pagan festivals became new Christian ones, and their old customs and ways of thought continued but little altered. Their greatest stumbling-block had been the incarnation. They could not see how God could become incarnate, but they were quite ready to accept the incarnation of a subordinate divine being. Their mythology and literature were full of instances of semi-divine heroes, like Hercules, living among men, and they did not feel any instinctive objection to the Christ of Arius. He fitted their thought-forms, their mental climate, better than did the profounder and more mysterious Christ of Athanasius. The Arian tendency towards polytheism did not disturb them. It made their break with paganism that much easier, just as half a

THE BATTLE WITH ARIANISM

journey is easier than a whole-way journey. Arianism was plainer, simpler, more adapted to unsophisticated minds. It is not strange, therefore, that Goths and Lombards and Huns adopted and clung to this form of Christianity, and that it made a powerful appeal to the new converts everywhere. It was just there that the gravest danger lay.

The struggle over Arianism proved to be one of the greatest contests in the Christian Church, and the fierceness, the bitterness and the hate engendered showed little enough of the spirit of the Galilean. It is a long way across the centuries to a little simple poem by G. K. Chesterton, which expresses how easy it is to lose the plain way of life amid the complexities and confusions which we " wise men " make :

> " Step softly, under snow or rain,
> To find the place where men can pray :
> The way is all so very plain
> That we may lose the way.
>
> " Oh, we have learnt to peer and pore
> On tortured puzzle from our youth,
> We know all labyrinthine lore,
> We are the three Wise Men of yore,
> And we know all things but the truth.
>
> " Go humbly : humble are the skies,
> And low and large and fierce the Star :
> So very near the manger lies
> That we may travel far."

That the orthodox view was forged out into the final form and eventually prevailed was due, in the main, to the persistent and valiant championship of

THE CHURCH'S DEBT TO HERETICS

one man, Athanasius (300–373)—*Athanasius contra mundum*. He saw clearly that if Christ is only a creature, however exalted, then He is not truly God ; neither can He show God to us nor bring us into union with Him. His overmastering and dominating idea was the incarnation. God and Christ are one as the fountain and the river are one, as the sun and the radiance from it are one, as the mind and its intelligent purposes are one. Christ is literally and truly a God-Man. He is a double revelation. He is God by nature, and He makes God clearly known, and at the same time He is the Head of the new order of humanity, and as such He reveals man's true nature and constitution. " He has become Man that we might be raised to a Divine life." [1]

Nature, the created world, shows us nothing which can deliver us from sin or death. In one who is like ourselves God has come to us, has shown Himself to us, has conquered death and sin, puts the power of victory within our reach, and makes it possible for us to participate in His triumphant life. Athanasius cared less for logic than Arius did. He built much more naturally upon experience. He had *felt* the unparalleled significance of the incarnation. It throbbed and beat in his own soul, and he was resolved not to let it be emptied of its transforming power by the dry processes of syllogism. Here were two types of men, and their two groups of followers were marked with similar characteristics of mind and

[1] *De incar.*, sec. 44.

THE BATTLE WITH ARIANISM

spirit. Those who followed in the great struggle did very little individual thinking. They were attracted by personalities, by general slogans, by broad types of Christianity. Athanasius had great spiritual depth—depth of feeling, as well as of intellect. He approached his religious problem from a basis of experience. He *lived* his way into the meaning of Christ's revelation, and he *saw*, as a mystic sees, the truths of which he wrote or spoke. He had a clear intellect, a broad range of thought, but he entered regions also to which logic had no key.

Arius, on the other hand, arrived at his positions by dialectic. He had a scientific temper of mind. He disliked fringes and shadows. The edges of thought must be sharp and clear. He had no interest in mystic depths, nor in vague suggestions of realms beyond the margins of sure-footed thought. Athanasius, moreover, was a saint; Arius was an ascetic. In one particular they were both agreed. They both drew a sharp line between this world and the divine realm. Everybody did that, and we may as well, once for all, point out here how the double-world theory of the age affected the entire question of Christ's nature. This world and all its furnishings were " natural," the heavenly realm and all its choir were " supernatural." The sky divided and completely separated the two realms. Nothing which originated here below could ever become divine, while everything above the sky was inherently divine, though, even there, not everything was eternal and uncreated. Both Arius and Athanasius agreed that if the divine were ever to be found in this world it must come hither from beyond the sky. What they disagreed about was, whether in that divine realm above us only God was eternal and uncreated, as Arius thought, or whether Christ, as well as God, was eternal too, as Athanasius believed. In either case we are dealing with mysteries which are quite foreign to the Gospels, and upon which we have no sure word of prophecy. It is a debate of the fourth century, not of the first, nor, indeed, of the twentieth.

The Emperor proved to be a decisive factor in the controversy. Without his intervention the debate would in time have worn itself out, as so many previous debates had done. But Constantine found it necessary for his own purposes to end the hot discussions, and to bring the Church to a unity. He knew the perils of division, and having joined the Church, at least partly, for the sake of unifying his vast empire, he could not quietly sit still and see it shatter itself to pieces over an impractical mystery. He was a great statesman, a far-seeing man in the realm of affairs, though he was never at home in the intricate issues of the spirit, the problems of which he attacked as a piece of imperial politics.

At first he sent a representative to Alexandria with a letter telling Bishop Alexander and Arius that they were engaged in a mere word-battle, discussing abstractions and petty trifles, and that they should

THE BATTLE WITH ARIANISM

adjust their differences. The letter produced no calm; it rather increased the storm, and forthwith Constantine took the decisive step of calling all the bishops, inside and outside the Empire, to a Council to make an end of the controversy and to restore unity. The Council met at Nicæa, "the city of victory," in Bithynia, in the summer of 325. According to tradition there were 318 bishops in the Council, many of them "confessors" during the preceding persecution, who still bore in their body the marks of their faith. Some had lost hands or feet, and some had had an eye plucked out. The Arians, counting on the timidity of the rural bishops and on the influence of the Emperor's half-sister, Constantia, had expected to make a very strong showing in the Council, but from the first onset they found themselves hopelessly beaten. The trouble came when the orthodox party undertook the adoption of a creed which would make the Arians *stay* beaten. The Arian party was eager for a creed expressed entirely in Scripture phrases, for such a creed would have been vague, indefinite and ambiguous, *i.e.*, capable of more than one interpretation; but Athanasius, who was not a member of the Council, though a great power behind the scenes, was determined to secure a creed that could mean only one thing for everybody.

Eusebius of Cæsarea, the Church historian, a moderate sympathiser with the Arian position, proposed the adoption of the creed of his own Church

THE CHURCH'S DEBT TO HERETICS

at Cæsarea : " We believe in God, the Father Almighty, Maker of all things both visible and invisible ; and in one Lord Jesus Christ, the Word of God, God from God, Light from Light, Life from Life, the only-begotten Son, the first-born of all creation, begotten of the Father before all ages, by whom all things were made ; who for our salvation was made flesh, and lived among men and suffered and rose again the third day and ascended to the Father, and shall come again in glory to judge quick and dead ; and in the Holy Ghost."

The Arians blundered by eagerly assenting to this creed. Athanasius and his friends did not want a creed which the Arian sympathisers liked. It was, however, adopted, and then amended so as to remove all ambiguities from it. " First-born of all creation " might mean that there was a time when He began to be ; " begotten before all worlds " might be construed to imply " created " ; " was made flesh " did not settle the question of His divinity or His humanity. After the words " one Lord Jesus Christ," they added " Son of God, begotten of the Father, that is of the essence of the Father," using the Greek word οὐσία for essence, or substance ; and after the words " Light from Light," they added " true God from true God ; begotten, not made, being of the same essence as the Father." Here was introduced the famous word " homoousios " (" of the same essence "). The word was not newly coined for the occasion. It was a favourite word of

THE BATTLE WITH ARIANISM

the Sabellians, and Eusebius of Nicomedia had said earlier in the Council that if the orthodox party insisted that Christ was "uncreated," that would mean that He was "homoousios," which, he supposed, none of them would wish to say, as that would be Sabellian. But the word was at once boldly seized upon—" I thank thee, Jew, for teaching me that word "—and was finally inserted, no doubt at the instigation of Athanasius, who was determined to have a creed that maintained the eternity of Christ and His oneness with God. In pushing the creed over to this extreme position he took great risks of forcing a later reaction, and he threw out the most defiant challenge to the party of the left, a challenge which was very sure to be accepted, as he was soon to discover. All but two of the bishops, however, finally signed the creed. These two, with Arius, were sent into exile, and the rest went home, supposing that the portentous heresy was wiped out, never to reappear.

Gradually, contrary to all expectation, an immense reaction, an unpredictable turn of events, set in, and a new and more dangerous stage of the controversy emerged. To understand the strange shifts and turns of the current during the lifetime of Athanasius one would need to know fully the complex spirit and temper of the age, the mental and moral habits of the people, and the intricate political schemes of the imperial circle. Society was heathen to the core, crude, sordid and confused, and the Church was then, as always, made up of people ! There were great souls in it ; pure, noble women, and high-minded, saintly men, but there were large masses of men and women who carried on the customs and habits of their old way of life and who were Christian only in name. The Emperors' courts were full of plotting, scheming courtiers and favourites, and the decisions of history were sometimes shaped by wise foresight and statesmanship and sometimes by sheer caprice and whimsical ambition.

What was needed most was a real interpretation and dissemination of the Gospel of Christ, a fresh experiment of His way of life, a practical application of the Kingdom of God. Instead of that there were exhibited all the disintegrating forces of hate and bitterness, a constant spectacle of border warfare between the men who were supposed to be the pillar Christians of the time. Christianity seemed to consist of fine-drawn and abstract definitions of dim, remote, other-world realities. Instead of having a loving, sympathising, sin-forgiving Saviour, who touched their lives and understood all their needs, those who flocked to the churches heard of a shadowy being whose metaphysical relation to God was the absorbing question. Instead of feeling the warm and tender enveloping and invading presence of the invisible Christ, the Life of all intimate spiritual experience, they heard endless discussions about generated and ungenerated existences.

It is a partial explanation of the pitiful fact that

THE BATTLE WITH ARIANISM

Christianity had not yet been tried on a large scale. It is one sad instance of the immemorial habit of substituting a rationalistic debate for a religious experience.

The reaction against the Nicene Creed began with a conservative dislike for the new words which had been introduced into it. They were unfamiliar and unscriptural words. They were difficult to explain and interpret, and it proved to be almost impossible to translate them into exact equivalents in other languages, even into Latin. Then there was a real feeling on the part of many that the new creed favoured the Sabellian heresy. Furthermore, the Imperial family, from the days of Constantine to Julian, was at heart Arian, while Constantius, Constantine's son and successor, worked and schemed to make the Empire positively Arian. Little by little a multitude of parties formed around various religious leaders, dominant personalities, political figures, or ecclesiastical dignitaries. These parties soon became vortexes of the most ominous sort, swirling centres of thought and action. Athanasius was four times exiled from his city and as many times restored again in the sudden shifts of fortune. Hilary of Poitiers, Hosius of Cordova, Meletius of Lycopolis, Marcellus of Ancyra, were some of the storm centres in this ever-changing theological drift.

The Arians themselves became hopelessly divided, too, after the death of Arius (336), which was believed by many at the time to have been a direct supernatural stroke. An extreme left movement developed, called the Anomœan heresy. It was ultra-Arian, frank and unevasive. The leaders of this movement plainly said that Christ was a " creature " and " essentially unlike " God, though revealing a *moral* resemblance to Him. The semi-Arian —a moderate movement—was the most important of all the opposing parties. The battle cry of this party was the word " Homoiousios," by which they meant that Christ was of a *similar* essence, or substance, with the Father. The struggle between the *Homoousian* party and the *Homoiousian* party gave Gibbon the ground for his famous jest that the whole controversy was a contest over a single diphthong ! Finally there was a third section which contended for mere *likeness* of character between Christ and the Father, without any reference to essence, *i.e.*, substantial likeness. These Arians were called Homœans. It was a confused noise of battle and tumult, and the forces surged now one way and now another, without much promise that a real solution would ever arrive. On the whole, the reign of the Emperor Julian (361–363) helped to bring the final solution and materially favoured the orthodox wing of the Church. He was a man of heroic spirit and noble temper. He blundered at many points and tried the impossible, but at least he had a pure and lofty purpose. He had seen only a travesty of Christianity, and from *that* he revolted. He was not an " apostate," he was an honest seeker, only he failed

THE BATTLE WITH ARIANISM

to find anything great enough to be a world religion. His intense championship of the old Greek religion and of Neo-Platonic philosophy rallied the Christian forces together to an unexpected degree, closed up their ranks and submerged petty local issues. When Julian died, from a chance Persian arrow in 363, the orthodox forces found themselves much more compact and unified than at any time since the Nicene Council, and Julian's traditional words, " Thou hast conquered, O Galilean," seemed on the way to be fulfilled. Not long after (373) Athanasius died, with a Pisgah vision of triumph in his eyes. Meantime the Empire was engaged in a life-and-death struggle with new races and new issues. The terrible defeat of Valens' army at the Battle of Adrianople in 378 flashed the handwriting on the wall before the eyes of all who could see the meaning of things. The Church now began in earnest to gird itself for moral and spiritual leadership as the visible Empire crumbled. Theodosius, the victorious Emperor of the West, in 380 took baptism, proclaimed his allegiance to the orthodox faith and ordered the Bishops to conform. The three great Cappadocian Fathers of this period, Basil, Gregory of Nyssa and Gregory of Nazianzus, exercised a commanding spiritual influence and did much to produce a new and better era for the Church. In 381 the Second General Council (Constantinople) confirmed the Nicene faith, and two years later, Arianism was proscribed and proclaimed illegal for Roman citizens. This was

THE CHURCH'S DEBT TO HERETICS

not quite its end, for the work of the great Arian missionary to the Goths, Bishop Ulfilas, had proved to be very effective, and these, and other conquering races, continued for many generations to follow a form of Arian faith.

It is not possible to speak with much enthusiasm of positive contributions which the Arian heresies made to the Church. It can, perhaps, be said that the Arian Christianity was closer to the mental level of the masses who were at this time entering the Church, closer also to the mental level of the new tribes and races that were just then surging over the frontiers of the Empire and preparing for the next great act in the human drama. It is possible that many accepted this simpler form of faith who would have refused a more exalted one. But if it was a simple form that was desired, there was at hand already a much better simple form than the Arian, namely, that presented in the Gospels. It is impossible now to make a good defence of Arianism. It was a thin, poor makeshift for Christianity. It was a low stage of moral insight, a crude interpretation of Christ, and it was for the most part championed by shifty, evasive, time-serving men, who lacked virile character and moral earnestness.

What can be successfully claimed is a fair negative contribution. The long, hard fight did result in a deep and serious facing of the question of Christ's real nature. In that critically momentous epoch, when the Empire was ostensibly surrendering to the

THE BATTLE WITH ARIANISM

Church, but when really the Empire was more or less adopting and absorbing the Church, it was worth something to have Christians forced to fight, to fight *in extremis*, for spiritual issues—not for land and endowments, but for the divine nature of its Founder and its Head. It was no small achievement to get the matter settled once for all that even if God be nowhere else present in person in this world, He was at least substantially present in Christ. That was what Athanasius stood for against the world, and, when the mists of battle cleared, Athanasius had won.

CHAPTER V

HERESIES OF THE HUMAN

" Human, all too Human "

WE have been following the great struggle of the Church to affirm the absolutely divine nature of Christ. In this long contest the opponents of the Church were weak because they were the champions of a Christ neither truly human nor truly divine. No great thinker, no real spiritual genius, could have been satisfied with the Christ of Arius. That Christ was doomed to fail, if the race progressed, because men were sure to outgrow such an artificially constructed Christ.

A more dangerous rival to the Christ of the Nicene Creed and of Athanasius would have been a Christ who was in every sense human, and who found a way to rise by divine help from His truly human nature to full unity and complete sonship with God. That is the course which the Eastern heresies next took. We meet now a strong tendency to glorify and exalt human nature. It is in some degree a contra-reaction against the dogma of original sin and depravity, but that does not wholly account for the movement. It was, at least, partly due to the fact that the men with whom this chapter deals were pure and lofty moral characters of the " once-born " type. They

HERESIES OF THE HUMAN

felt and experienced, more than most others, the far-reaching possibilities of human nature, and they believed that the theological accounts of man were for the most part travesties of it, not true descriptions of it.

I shall deal, in a single chapter, with two quite diverse phases of the tendency, one Eastern and the other Western; one concerned primarily with Christ and the other with man and human freedom. But they are at bottom close together. The leaders of the two movements felt their kinship, and their opponents naturally linked them together in a common condemnation. Antioch, where the followers of Christ were first called Christians, was the centre of one of the movements, and Britain, or perhaps Ireland, was the birthplace of the leader of the other one.

One of the most interesting and lovable of all the early Christian scholars was that devout and saintly man and brilliant writer known in history as Theodore of Mopsuestia. He was born in Antioch in 350, of a highly gifted family. He himself was possessed of great natural gifts, and, in addition, he received the best education available in his day. He had teachers renowned for scholarship and saintliness, and among his fellow-students were some of the noblest men of that age. He formed a very intimate friendship with John, later called Chrysostom, "the golden-mouthed," and with Maximus, who became Bishop of Seleucia. At the age of eighteen, under the influence of Chrysostom, Theodore renounced a secular career and dedicated himself to the religious life, which meant a life separated from the world. He had, however, in his early youth, become attached to a beautiful maiden named Hermione, whom he could not forget. Under the powerful appeal of her love he resolved to leave the ascetic life and " return to the world." His friend Chrysostom was deeply distressed by this tendency to lapse, and he wrote him two famous letters, *Ad Theodorum lapsum*, which called him back to his original resolution. One of the letters says : " It was as you were leaving the harbour, not as you were bringing home your vessel laden, that this dread pirate fell upon you."

John's powerful appeal brought him back to his spiritual dedication, and, when once his mind was settled and the die was cast, he flung himself with tremendous zeal into the religious and intellectual mission which he had chosen. He made himself a master of " divine learning." His first important work of exegesis was *A Commentary on the Psalms*. It revealed a new type of scholarship. It was historical and critical in character, and opposed to the allegorical method of interpretation in vogue in Alexandria. He set himself strongly against the traditional Messianic interpretation of the Psalms. Even now the work has a strangely modern cast. He was not afraid of " pagan " scholarship, and he drew liberally upon the exact and scientific methods of the Greek schools of the period, but his heart was

HERESIES OF THE HUMAN

sound, and his Christian faith and practice were pure and uncompromising. He was ordained at about the age of forty, and entered upon his life of public ministry with almost unparalleled promise. He was made Bishop of Mopsuestia, a town in Paul's Cilicia, which was a place of considerable importance in the fourth century. Constantine constructed a famous bridge there over the Pyramus. The city, once so important, is now an insignificant town named Mensis, near Adana.

Theodore was invited to preach before the Emperor, Theodosius I., in 395, on which occasion both his personality and his preaching made a profound impression. The Emperor declared with emphasis that he had never before met such a preacher. But great as he was with his voice, he was even greater with his pen. He became the most famous representative of the Antioch school of exegetical writers. He wrote Commentaries on almost every book of the Bible. They followed the track already marked out by his study of the Psalms. He insisted on discovering the literal meaning of the book rather than its allegorical meaning; and, secondly, he always aimed to find the historical background and setting of the book in hand. He refused to read an assumed spiritual meaning back into a passage. He always asked first of all, what did these words mean to the man who wrote them, and what significance did they have for their original readers. He questioned the common tendency of the time to find far-fetched prophecies of Christ in words that were open to a more obvious interpretation. He is thus an opponent of Origen's method, and is a saner and more rational type of exegete, though he does not stir the enthusiasm of his reader to the same pitch, and he consequently produces fewer thrills. He assumes that there are varying degrees of inspiration revealed in the books of Scripture. The books of wisdom-literature, usually attributed to Solomon, are put by him on a low level of inspiration. He calls the Song of Solomon a nuptial poem—and not a spiritual allegory, as everybody else thought it to be. He rejected Ezra, Nehemiah and Chronicles as not genuine parts of the canon of Scripture. He eliminated the titles to the Psalms, and declared the reputed authors mentioned in these titles have only the weight of unverified tradition. He rejected the Epistle of James, which a later critic, Martin Luther, called " a right strawy epistle," and he freely criticised other books of the Bible. He lacked, of course, the sound critical methods of modern scholarship, but he had the *spirit* which we should now call " modern," and he felt the full importance of approaching a book with historical insight. It is, however, his Christology, and not his exegesis, that mainly concerns us. In this he is a follower, though a free and creative one, of Paul of Samosata. He formulated his position in marked opposition to Apollinarius of Laodicea, whom Harnack calls " perhaps the most acute and far-seeing theologian of the century." The latter maintained that there were two complete natures in the incarnate Christ. Apollinarius was a sympathetic follower of Aristotle, a keen psychologist, and a clear, logical thinker. He was especially interested in thinking through the psychological nature of Christ. He saw no way to unite in a single individual the absolute God and the full psychological nature of man. He therefore came to the conclusion that Christ had a human body and a human soul (*i.e.*, human life and human senses), but in place of the normal rational nature of a man He had within Him the Logos of God. Like Arius, Apollinarius presented a Christ neither fully human nor fully divine, but "a certain middle something." Instead of a real incarnation of God we have a " contrivance " to solve the *impasse*— the problem of showing how perfect God and perfect man could unite in a single person. Apollinarius did his intellectual best to find a " way out," but really found none. He made one point clear, however, that nobody could deal profoundly with the problem of Christ's nature without being regarded a heretic from one side or the other.

Against Apollinarius, Theodore held emphatically to the complete manhood of Christ and the perfection of His human experience. The Logos, he believed, was pre-existent, but when He became incarnate in Christ Jesus He assumed complete and perfect manhood, and underwent the normal stages of ethical and spiritual development, like any other person.

THE CHURCH'S DEBT TO HERETICS

Throughout His earthly life Christ's humanity was real and genuine, though the Divine Logos, who dwelt in Him, raised Him to an unwonted spiritual power and enabled Him to perform an extraordinary mission of service and salvation.

Theodore, with his genius for interpretation, clearly caught the meaning and spirit of St. Paul's conception of Christ as a new Adam, the beginner of a new order of humanity, a race of spiritual men. Christ is thus a new Creation, the first-fruits of a higher order. Christ, for Theodore, is not a *dual* being, with two natures, two selves conjoined. He is one unique being. Christ was tempted, really tempted as we are, He struggled and grappled with emotions, passions and instincts, but He triumphed. He became victorious and passed over into a state of complete purity and invincible virtue. The victory was due to the indwelling of God in Him. Many saints, before and since, have had divine assistance, and have arrived at a lofty stage of holiness, but they have not reached His height. Christ possessed in a unique degree a moral and spiritual nature which fitted Him for an unusual and transcending gift of divine indwelling and assistance, and He thereby rose to the complete sharing of the life of God and to the full dignity of sonship with God. He became morally and spiritually one with God—one with Him in heart and mind, in will and spirit. His life was a life through which the full nature and character of God could be revealed to men.

HERESIES OF THE HUMAN

At the same time Theodore had a very much greater respect for human nature than his contemporaries had. Christ's life and His moral triumph were signal indications of the immense possibilities of man. Christ was both God and man, and He has revealed the natures of both. Theodore strongly emphasised the point, later taught by Pelagius, that man's sin is due to decision of will, not to man's corrupt and depraved nature. Man is captain of his soul. He holds the moral tiller, and he may sin or not as he chooses.

Theodore lived and died unsuspected of heresy. He was believed in and loved by the greatest preacher of his age—some would say of any age—John Chrysostom, the golden-mouthed apostle of truth ; he was beloved and approved, too, by some of the greatest and best men of his time, but in a later period his works were found to be breeders of heresy. They were brought under suspicion because heretics loved them ! Cyril, the supreme champion of orthodoxy in a later controversy, which in course we must study, turned all his high-power guns on Theodore's writings.[1]

If it had not been for the stir made by Nestorius, it is probable that, " after life's fitful fever," Theodore of Mopsuestia would have slept undisturbed, and it is further probable that Nestorius would have

[1] The final official condemnation of Theodore's writings was pronounced at the Fifth General Council, held at Constantinople in 553. This anathema was drawn up under the influence of the Emperor Justinian, who, as Hefele says, had " a mania for dogmatizing."

THE CHURCH'S DEBT TO HERETICS

finished his course in peace if it had not been for the heresy-hunting spirit—what has been called " the tyrannous orthodoxy "—of Cyril, Patriarch of Alexandria. Nestorius was born in a small town of Syria, and he was baptised and educated in Antioch. The exact date of his birth cannot be settled, but he became Archbishop and Patriarch of Constantinople in 428. His appointment to this exalted position was made for political reasons, and his later troubles were due in large measure to political complications. He visited Theodore of Mopsuestia on his way to Constantinople, and the latter, then already near his death, and touched with a spirit of gentleness, warned Nestorius not to be so hot against the opinions of others. He, however, soon forgot the wise advice of the old teacher, and on the occasion of his consecration sermon he said to the Emperor: " Give me the earth purged of heretics, and I will repay you with heaven." He proceeded at once to carry out this policy of zeal, and his strenuous procedure accumulated much of the hostility with which he had to reckon later. He must many times have reflected upon his measures of suppression when his own turn came, as a greater Christian before his day reflected.

The troubles began from a sermon preached by Anastasius, domestic chaplain of Nestorius, in the autumn of this same year of consecration. In the course of the sermon Anastasius denied that the Virgin Mary was rightly called " Theotokos "—

HERESIES OF THE HUMAN

"Mother of God." "Let no one," he said, "call Mary Mother of God; for Mary was but human, and it is impossible for God to be born of human kind."[1] This phrase had become a popular one, and the attack upon it seemed to many a scandal, but Nestorius heartily sympathised with his chaplain's position, and proceeded to back it up with all the force of his great eloquence. He believed that the phrase was thoroughly unchristian, and he was especially opposed to it because it was a favourite word of Apollinarius, who seemed to Nestorius an arch-heretic. In a series of sermons begun on Christmas Day, 428, he flung himself with great earnestness against the use of the hated word. He declared that it was absurd to call any finite person "the Mother of God," or to intimate that God was born and "wrapped in swaddling clothes and laid in a manger." He contended that the custom of using the word was an unfortunate relic of paganism. He pointed out that even Melchizedek was "without father, without mother, without descent," how much more ought that to be true of one to whom we give the name God. "That which is born of flesh is flesh, and that which is born of spirit is spirit. Call not, then, Mary, Mother of God"!

There was tremendous excitement over the Christmas sermon. Nestorius was protested against on the spot, the clergy and the members of the religious orders became furious opponents, though the

[1] The sermon is reported by Socrates, *Eccl. Hist.*, B. VII., chap. 32.

THE CHURCH'S DEBT TO HERETICS

Imperial court supported him. His other sermons in the series were more restrained, but the storm had begun, and it would not grow quiet. Proclus, an aspiring cleric, who was later to take the place occupied by Nestorius, followed up the series of sermons with a powerful eulogium on the Virgin Mary, calling her " Mother of God," and closing with an eloquent peroration at which the immense audience burst into applause. Nestorius was present and rose at once to his feet and replied in a remarkable extempore address. This was followed later with a carefully prepared reply to Proclus, in which Nestorius said : " I have learned from Scripture that God passed through the Virgin Mother of Christ ; that God was born of her I have never learned." At this point Cyril, Patriarch of Alexandria, stirred up the waters with an added breeze. He was ambitious to be leader of the Eastern Church as he was already the august leader of the Egyptian Church. He wrote an open letter, addressed to the monks of Egypt, defending the use of the phrase " Theotokos," as applied to Mary. Mother of Christ, he said, is not a great enough word, for she bore not a godlike man, but an incarnate God. Meantime the Pope, Celestine, heard of the controversy, and wrote to Cyril for information about Nestorius' position, and from this point onward the correspondence and the entanglement became too complicated to be dealt with in my brief account. There was plain and obvious rivalry between the two

HERESIES OF THE HUMAN

seats—that of Constantinople and Alexandria—and Cyril was not concerned with the high matters of orthodoxy alone : he wanted to humble a rival. Cyril moved every known influence to overwhelm Nestorius. He kept the pot boiling by constantly adding fuel to the flame. He pulled the strings of influence at Rome, and he fed fat every jealousy that showed itself against Nestorius in Constantinople. His main motive may have been love of truth and desire to promote spiritual progress, but one suspects that there were at least other sub-motives mixed in with the pure one.

Nestorius on his part felt that he was fighting once more the battle against paganism. He saw, or thought he saw, in the glorification of the Virgin, an attempt to treat her as a goddess to be worshipped, and he was resolved to check that worship. At the same time he felt that Cyril's Christ, like the Christ of Apollinarius, was an abstraction, without any true nature and character, either divine or human. Cyril seemed to him to blur over or to eliminate altogether the humanity of Christ. Cyril, he noted, never referred in his correspondence to Christ's human nature. Nestorius himself was endeavouring to interpret Christ in such a way as to keep both the divine and the human natures. There was, he insisted, one incarnation, one Person, one Christ, but two natures blended, without surrender or confusion, into one complete revelation of God and man. Mary is not *theotokos*, the Mother of God ; she is Christotokos, the Mother of Christ. Mary did not bear the Godhead, she bore a man who was the inseparable instrument or organ of divinity. Nestorius is plainly a member of the school of Antioch. His Christology, as Harnack says, is that of Theodore, and he clearly shows the influence of Chrysostom. He will not admit that God can have an origin, a beginning, or that He can grow and change, nor will he consent to a conception of Christ which does not in the fullest measure maintain His complete humanity. He presented, or endeavoured to present, a Christ in whom two perfect natures—the divine and the human—were united indivisibly in one Person. At any moment, in the early stages of the controversy, Nestorius might have saved himself from the heretic's fate if he would have consented to use, or to approve the use of, the crucial word, but he would not do it, and the endless debates only drove the two sides farther apart and caused each leader to formulate a more extreme position than he occupied at first. Cyril formulated twelve anathemas which he endeavoured to get Nestorius to sign, the first one of which said: "If any one shall assert that Emmanuel is not very God, and consequently that His blessed Mother is not the Mother of God, let him be anathema."

In 430 a Council met in Rome and considered the Nestorian tangle. The Pope had by this time come to an understanding with Cyril and was on his side. He wrote to Cyril thanking him for his watchfulness and faithfulness. At the same time he wrote to Nestorius in this ominous fashion : " If you do not preach concerning Christ our God the things which the Roman, the Alexandrian, and the whole Catholic Church hold, nay, which the Church of Constantinople has hitherto held—and if you do not condemn, publicly and in writing, your novel doctrines within ten days from the receipt of this admonition, you will be cast out from the communion of the Catholic Church."

Nestorius was as firm as a rock and resolved not to yield, feeling certain in his mind that a General Council would support him. He counted much upon the great influence of the Bishop of Antioch, which he felt sure would be on his side. This expected Council was called to meet in Ephesus in 431. A large number of bishops, including the Bishop of Antioch, failed to arrive at the time set for the opening of the Council. Cyril, however, declared that the 159 bishops who were present constituted a genuine Council. The Emperor sent a messenger protesting against holding the Council until the others arrived, and Nestorius and his friends refused to recognise its authority. Cyril, however, who presided, at once proceeded to anathematise Nestorius, and to pronounce his teaching impious and heretical. At the time of final action the Council had increased to the number of 198, all of whom signed the sentence of deposition and excommunication.

THE CHURCH'S DEBT TO HERETICS

In his Apology Nestorius wrote : " Who assembled the Council ? Cyril. Who was its head ? Cyril. Who was judge ? Cyril. And who the accuser ? Cyril. Who the Bishop of Rome ? Cyril. Cyril was everything."

One cannot feel that Nestorius was a saint, or that he was free from blame for the miserable situation which did so much to weaken the life and power of the Church at this epoch, but, on the other hand, it must be said that he was a brave and honest man, fighting a real fight which he believed was the urgent battle of the faith for his time. He saw Christianity being paganised, and he believed that the tendency to regard Mary as the Mother of God was one of the major errors of that time. There was a stormy period of a few years before Cyril and John of Antioch were reconciled to each other, but eventually, after many failures to agree, they came to a peaceable understanding, and John signed a confession of faith which satisfied Cyril. Harnack calls this " union " the " saddest and most momentous event " " since the condemnation of Paul of Samosata."[1] Cyril was the winning exponent of a Christianity which was a very close approach to what was later called Monophysitism, or Eutychianism (named after Eutyches), the heresy that in Christ there was only one nature and that nature Divine. Cyril held that as God dwelt in the burning bush without consuming the bush, so Divine Nature appropriated

[1] *Hist. of Dog.*, IV., p. 197.

HERESIES OF THE HUMAN

human nature without partaking in any way of its weaknesses. Christ was one Person and that Person Divine. Cyril was always skating on thin ice, and only by juggling with words and thus concealing his inconsistencies did he avoid falling into one or the other of the opposing heresies. In fact Eutychianism is only a slight expansion of Cyril's views.

Nestorius withdrew from the storms of life after his deposition and resided in the quiet monastery near Antioch where he had been a brother before his elevation. The Emperor banished him to Petra and then to the great Oasis in Egypt. He was hounded by enemies and maltreated by robbers, driven from place to place, badly injured by a fall, suffering from disease, and finally relieved from trouble by kindly death about 451. There is a tradition that his grave is never visited by the dews of heaven!

His own *Nunc Dimittis* is given in his Apology : " As for me, I have borne the sufferings of my life and all that has befallen me in this world as the sufferings of a day ; and I have not changed, lo, all these years, and now, lo, I am already on the point of departing, and daily I pray to God to dismiss me —me whose eyes have seen His salvation. Rejoice with me, O Desert, thou my friend and my up-bringer and my place of sojourning, and thou Exile, my mother, who after death shall keep my body until the resurrection cometh in the time of God's good pleasure. Amen."[1] According to all existing and

[1] Nestorius' Apology was written under the title *The Book of Heraclides*.

THE CHURCH'S DEBT TO HERETICS

approved standards of faith Nestorius was an orthodox Christian. He held the Nicene doctrine and was almost a fanatic in defence of its position. He was ready to go as far as Athanasius in maintenance of the *divinity of Christ*. He himself said, with justice, that Basil, and Gregory, and Athanasius, and Ambrose, would all come under the same condemnation which had fallen upon him.

He was ready to assert that Christ was born of a Virgin, but he would not call her " Mother of God." He had the major *rôle* in a real tragedy. He was a well-trained scholar, an impressive teacher, a good administrator, a faithful pastor of his flock ; he was not an innovator, but rather a conservative follower of the line of noble interpreters of Antioch who were dedicated to the task of keeping firm hold of the fact that Christ lived among men a genuinely human life. If he had not had the misfortune to come into collision with a heresy-hunter of the first rank he would have finished his career with fame and glory and the Church would have been spared one of its saddest chapters. Nestorius was abandoned by his most prominent friends and left to his hard fate, not because these friends thought him a heretic or that they were changed to Cyril's views, but because they took the course of safety and ran to shelter. Nestorius stood for a purer and loftier Christianity than that which his conquerors professed. He saw the danger which threatened from the immense popular growth of the cult of the Virgin, and he endeavoured

HERESIES OF THE HUMAN

to stem the rising current of enthusiasm for it, but he failed.

After Cyril and John of Antioch were reconciled and joined forces sterner measures were adopted against the followers of Nestorius. They were driven out of their positions and forced to retreat into Persia. The famous school in Edessa became for a time a centre of Nestorian thought and influence. This school was dissolved by the edict of the Emperor Zeno in 489. At a later date a still more effective intellectual centre for the training of Nestorian Christians was founded in Nisibis, and here Theodore of Mopsuestia, through his writings, became the great doctor of the faith. The sect flourished and had a long history in and about Damascus. An important Nestorian movement and a separate Nestorian Church flourished for centuries in Persia under the name of the Chaldean Church and took on some of the ideas and traits of the Zoroastrians. It was a nationalist movement there, and was tolerated and encouraged by the kings of Persia *because* it was a form of Christian faith rejected by the Romans. The Church in Persia was autonomous. This faith became strongly missionary and penetrated China in the seventh century, where the Nestorian missionaries set up the famous Nestorian monument. Bagdad became a centre of the Nestorian Church, and it had in the thirteenth century as many as twenty-five metropolitan sees. Tamerlane left it only a feeble remnant, though it is estimated that there are 150,000 in Kurdistan and Persia and 120,000 in India.

The Pelagian controversy brings us to a new stage, in fact, to a new level, in the discussion of the problems of Christian thought. We are at last in the West and not in the East, where the previous controversies had their habitat. This struggle was closely tied up with the so-called heresies of Theodore and Nestorius, but it had a very different centre of interest. It was more directly concerned with the fundamental nature of man, and it raised important psychological questions as well as theological ones. Pelagius belonged to that interesting strand of British Christianity which antedated the planting of Christianity at Canterbury by St. Augustine, the missionary to England. His birthplace cannot be determined. He is called a Briton, but that may mean, and probably does mean, a native of Ireland. He was born about 370. He came to Rome not far from the beginning of the fifth century—very likely in 401. He was a pure and holy man, as even St. Augustine of Hippo, his greatest opponent, admits. He was shocked at the laxity and weakness of the Church, as he found it in Rome, and he came to the conclusion that one reason for the low state of spiritual life was the prevailing theory that man possessed no power or capacity within himself for doing good. He expressed his own position in these bold words : " In dealing with ethics and the principles of a holy life, I first demonstrate the power to decide and act

HERESIES OF THE HUMAN

inherent in human nature and show what it can achieve, lest the mind be careless and sluggish in pursuit of virtue in proportion to its want of belief in its power, and in its ignorance of its attributes should think that it does not possess them." He shared with many other pure-minded Christians of the period a passion for withdrawal from the world, and he was thus an eager advocate of monastic holiness. He was a careful student, proficient in both Greek and Latin, a good writer, an excellent speaker, and he possessed an attractive and winning personality, though St. Jerome calls him "that great fat dog of Albion!" His main concern was the practical life, but he found himself quickly drawn into the field of hot theological controversy. He always remained at heart opposed to dogmas and opposed also to the formation of theological systems. His religion consisted, not in schemes of belief, but in a practical, positive Christian life. He deprecated theological discussions and only discussed problems himself because he felt forced to do so. The world was passing through one of the greatest crises in the long history of civilisation. The new races had emerged and were battering at the gates of the ancient capital, but nothing was able to draw men's minds away from the issues of theology. These questions were major questions, even though Rome was falling. Pelagius was roused to a strong pitch of opposition to the type of Christianity which St. Augustine, his greatest contemporary, was developing. He greatly disapproved of many statements in the *Confessions* and in his other writings of this period. The passage to which he most objected was the prayer of St. Augustine in the *Confessions* (X. 40), " Lord, Thou hast commanded continence ; give what Thou commandest and command what Thou wilt." This seemed to him to encourage a man to settle back into a lazy attitude and to wait for virtue until it might please God to confer and bestow it—" give what Thou commandest."

God seemed to him to be presented by the great African as an autocratic and almost tyrannical Being, not the Father that Christ had revealed. He himself was wholly in sympathy with the closer and tenderer relation between God and man as taught by Theodore of Mopsuestia, Chrysostom and Nestorius. He won to his side a clear-minded lawyer and rhetorician named Celestius, who, under his powerful example and influence, became a monk. Celestius dedicated himself to the holy life and set himself with Pelagius to the task of rousing a sluggish world to a higher faith and purer life. A third leader was found in Julian of Eclanum. It should be said in passing that Pelagius was more restrained and less " radical " than his followers were. They embarrassed him by their tendency to go to extremes, and they brought the new views into conflict with the authorities where he would have escaped if he had been involved alone. They were closer in type of mind to Aristotle than to Plato. They believed very strongly in the scope and power of human reason, and their warm sympathy with Stoic philosophy inclined them to emphasise the direct relationship between the human and the divine. Religion and moral goodness belong, they insisted, inherently to man's normal nature, and they set their views positively against the extreme view of the " fall," of man's depraved and abjectly sinful condition and his absolute need of divine Grace, doctrines which St. Augustine was forging out at this time. Both leaders, the Bishop of Hippo and the British monk, built primarily upon their own experience. The former had been plucked as a brand from the burning by what seemed an act of God's Grace; the latter was a "once-born" man, naturally pure, and fine, and noble, and thus he had known no sharp crisis of conversion. Their rival theories of salvation spring out of this fundamental difference in their personal experience.

Pelagius found a remarkable saying of Christ's which called men to be " perfect "—perfect even as the heavenly Father is perfect, and he simply and naïvely assumed that Christ meant what He said, and that this marvellous attainment must, therefore, lie within our human possibilities. He declared that each new-born child is in the same condition Adam was in before he fell, and that in every case, now as then, the " fall " is due to the definite sin of each individual, and that sin itself is the result of an act of free will. He attributed the pessimistic theory of human nature as completely vitiated and depraved

THE CHURCH'S DEBT TO HERETICS

to the baleful influence of Manichæan doctrines—Augustine had been a Manichæan before his conversion—and Pelagius leaned far over to the extreme other side. He held that human nature is a creation of God, and, therefore, it cannot be the black, vile thing which the theologians were prone to make it. He stood forth as the defender of human nature and as a believer in the divine origin of little children—the little children of whom Jesus said: " Of such is the Kingdom of God." He refused to admit that sin can be transmitted. Sin, being, as it is, an act of will, springs and can spring only from the personal decision of a free individual. It follows, therefore, that man must possess free will and the power of free choice. He went still farther, and declared that it is possible for man to live without sin, and to attain to a state which is pure and perfect. He held much the same view of the victorious life that George Fox held in the seventeenth century. His doctrine of Grace was characteristically different from that of St. Augustine. Pelagius felt that the supreme mark of Grace was to be found in the native original endowments bestowed upon man ; in the possession of reason and free will, those superiorities which raise him above the brutes ; but, above all, in the gift of Jesus Christ, in His revelation of the unmerited love of God, in His life and death, in His Gospel and His example. Pelagius believed as strongly in Grace as his chief opponent did, only he looked for it in a different place. One looked

HERESIES OF THE HUMAN

for it in the sphere of the natural ; the other in the sphere of the supernatural. Pelagius had a "modern" outlook and habit of mind. For him Grace is infused into and through all that God has done in creation and in history. He felt little need of looking for magical interventions and for divine schemes to "restore" a ruined universe, since he did not believe it to be ruined. He would say that every creative act of God reveals Grace, every new-born child is a gift of Grace, every deed of heroic endeavour bears testimony to the fact of divine Grace. Christ is the Grace of God, become visible and vocal. The Holy Spirit is the continuous bearer of Grace to the inner life of man. Pelagius vigorously declared that the Grace of God, by which Christ came into the world to save sinners, is necessary not only every hour, or every moment, but for every act. But this in no way reached the sphere of Grace according to St. Augustine's conception of it. "Pelagius gainsays," St. Augustine declares, "the Grace of Christ whereby we are justified, *by insisting on the sufficiency of nature to work righteousness, provided only the will be present.*" [1] This seemed to the great theologian to be sheer naturalism.

These men, Pelagius and his disciples, stood for a Christianity, the main emphasis of which was the *moral* emphasis, rather than the theological. They insisted that the first question to ask about any

[1] Aug., *Nature and Grace*, XXV.

THE CHURCH'S DEBT TO HERETICS

theological system is, does it stand for a God who is morally good, and does it help men to be better men and to lead better lives ? If not, it is unsound theology. The rock on which they built was the moral reason of man, and they protested against a Christianity " in bondage to stupid and godless dogmas." They insisted that it is just as *natural* to be good as it is to be bad ; that holiness is as *natural* as sinfulness is. Christ came to show us the full, complete nature of God, to make us see the meaning and possibilities of life, and to give us spiritual vision and moral dynamic for pure and holy living. Quite naturally, Pelagius treated baptism, especially the baptism of infants, with a different emphasis, and gave it a different significance, than did the theologians of Grace. St. Augustine himself puts the two positions side by side as follows : " See what he [Pelagius] has said. In the case of an infant born in a place where it was not possible for him to be admitted to the baptism of Christ, and being overtaken with death without having had the bath of regeneration, Pelagius would absolve the unbaptised child and, in spite of the Lord's sentence, would open to him the Kingdom of Heaven. The Apostle, however, does not absolve him [the child] when he says : ' By one man sin entered into the world, and death by sin ; by which death passed upon all men, for that all have sinned.' Rightly, therefore, by virtue of that condemnation which runs throughout the mass [of mankind], is he not admitted into the kingdom of heaven, although he [the child] was not only not a Christian, but was unable to become one."[1]

Against Pelagius and his followers were pitted the two greatest theologians of the age, St. Augustine and St. Jerome. The battle was fought first at Rome; then in North Africa, where St. Augustine lived; then in Palestine, where St. Jerome lived; and, finally, in Rome again, where, between 418 and 422, Boniface was Pope. The controversy carried St. Augustine on to ever greater extremes in his views of sin and depravity, and to ever greater demands upon supernatural Grace. He produced a long list of anti-Pelagian tracts which set forth his mature position. Here we find a type of Christianity that despairs utterly of human nature, which is conceived as a complete mass of sin; that admits no shred of merit in any work or effort of man; and that opens only one hope of salvation, which is to be found when man in sheer faith throws himself on the mercy of God, and accepts Grace transmitted alone through the supernatural channels of the Church. So complete is the havoc of the fall, in St. Augustine's view, that all human free will is lost, and the very faith by which a man accepts the Grace won through Christ's merits is a divine gift. Those who have received the gift of such saving faith are the "elect"; those who have not received it are the non-elect, which means "damned." It is no

[1] Aug., *Nature and Grace*, IX., freely rendered.

THE CHURCH'S DEBT TO HERETICS

doubt true that Pelagius, and his more radical followers, held too mild and superficial a view of sin. They did not feel its tragic depths as the great African theologian did. They moved in a wholly different world of thought and experience. They were free from the taint of Manichæan dualism, and they found human nature to be a noble gift of God, and the constitution and capacities of the soul a glorious creation. They did not feel the need of a Church supplied with mysterious, magical, supernatural resources of Grace, for they believed that man needed education, wisdom, light and vision, rather than mystery, magic and miracle. But they failed, and St. Augustine won. Their movement received overwhelming condemnation at the Council of Constantinople in 431. Pelagius and Celestius from this time disappear from the pages of history, and Julian died in Sicily in 454, hated by the orthodox, but loved by the poor people, to whom he gave everything he possessed to save them from hunger.

The time was not ripe for the proclamation of faith in the divine capacities and endowments of human nature. Augustine, and not Pelagius, or Theodore, or Nestorius, spoke the word which fitted the mental temper and genius of the time, but these beaten and condemned heretics were the champions of ideas which are quick and vital in the modern world to-day.

CHAPTER VI

HERESIES CONCERNING THE SPIRIT

WHILE almost every Christian leader had a well-defined theory of the nature of Christ, and, particularly in the West, an equally specific theory of the origin of sin, very few had any carefully formulated doctrine of the Holy Spirit. The early creeds, though infallibly certain on other points, give us no information about the nature of the Spirit. They limit their declarations to the mere affirmation: "And I believe in the Holy Ghost." Some one at an early period interpolated into 1 John v., the seventh verse, "There are three that bear record in heaven, the Father, the Word, and the Holy Ghost; and these three are one." These words are first quoted in a tract by Priscillian,[1] in 380, but they are found in no important Greek MS. In any case, however they got into the Vulgate, these words were destined to work powerfully upon men's imagination and to exert a far-reaching influence. Sabellius had already laid the foundation, as we have seen, of a clearly marked trinitarian system, though the fact that he was a heretic tended to weaken the value and influence of his attempt to put the Holy Spirit on an equality with the Father and the Son. One of the strongest strands of influence toward the

---
[1] Priscillian was the first heretic to be put to death by the Church.

formation of trinitarian doctrine is to be found in the prevailing philosophy of the time, Neo-Platonism, which formed the intellectual environment of some of the most distinguished Christian thinkers. That philosophy was, throughout its entire history, decidedly trinitarian. Plotinus, when he was working out his three supreme realities, had no intention of furnishing material assistance to his Christian rivals, but there can be no question that he did make a major contribution to Christian thought.

There is, however, a far more important strand of influence than either the philosophical or the theological one. There was a great foundational stratum of actual *experience*. Something happened at Pentecost which made the tiny new-born Church certain of the reality of the Spirit. They were conscious of an invasion, an inrushing, or upwelling of divine Life and Power, and they passed over from a visible Head to an invisible Presence working in them and through them. They made little attempt to define this experience, but they assumed either that Christ Himself was spiritually present with them, or that He had sent, or shed abroad, the Spirit somewhat as had been the case with prophets of old. Peter took this latter view, as reported in Acts, and the fourth Gospel speaks emphatically of the Paraclete whom Christ promised to send. But as the early Christian groups ate their *agapé* together—their communion, or memorial, meal—they were conscious of Christ's living, though invisible, presence with them.

HERESIES CONCERNING THE SPIRIT

St. Paul makes this vital, inward, resident work of Christ the basis of his entire interpretation of Christianity. With him, once more, it was experience, and not doctrine, that formed the basis. Some power, some *dunamis* not himself, seemed plainly operating in him—" the power of God unto salvation." He makes no effort to think out a single consistent formulation of this great central experience. Sometimes it is God who *works in us*; sometimes it is Christ who works, or who is formed, in us; sometimes it is the Spirit or the Holy Spirit who works, or dwells in us, as in a temple. Occasionally, as in 2 Cor. iii. 17, he identifies Christ as the Spirit. It is quite evident that for him Christ is now thought of as an invisible divine Life and Power in immediate contact and relationship with men—God as an operative inward spiritual Power. Both in the primitive apostolic circle, and in the Ægean churches founded by St. Paul, there were certain positive and sensible evidences of the work of the Spirit; the two most common evidences being the gift of tongues (glossolalia) and the gift, or outpouring, of prophecy. The fullest and clearest account in the New Testament of these striking experiences is to be found in First Corinthians. Tongue-speaking, which was obviously ecstatic and automatic utterance, and thus marvellous rather than edifying and constructive, soon fell into disfavour and gradually waned away as a vanishing, disappearing performance. Prophecy was reckoned by St. Paul a more important gift—

THE CHURCH'S DEBT TO HERETICS

" I had rather speak five words with my understanding, that I might instruct others, than ten thousand words in a tongue " (1 Cor. xiv. 19).

Prophecy was rapt, inspired, spontaneous speaking in which the speaker felt that his message was given to him at the time and for the occasion. He believed that the Spirit possessed him and was speaking through him. The messages to the Churches in Revelation are good examples of it. The writer says : " I was in the Spirit on the Lord's day, and I heard a voice saying, What thou seest write in a book and send to the seven churches " (Rev. i. 10). In the ministry of prophecy the speaker was often raised to a level of wisdom which transcended his normal powers—he spoke better than he knew. He *sensed* in a flash of intuition the state and condition of the group, and often brought the whole meeting into a fused and unified life, as though they were all suddenly " baptised in one Spirit into one body " (1 Cor. xii.). At its best, coming as it did through great spiritual personalities, in this early high-tide period, prophecy was a powerful type of ministry ; it played an important part in the formation of early Christianity, and it made the presence and power of the Spirit seem very real.

But it quickly degenerated and fell to a lower level, though not as quickly as tongue-speaking did. It was a form of ministry that called for a peculiar, and more or less unstable, psychical type of person. So long as the enthusiasm was high and so long as

HERESIES CONCERNING THE SPIRIT

persons of great spiritual experience were the organs of it, it tended to organise and edify the life of the Church, but when the second and third generation came on the scene men of more ordinary gifts and thinner experience soon revealed the weakness of this type of ministry. It easily dropped to a low, poor quality, and became tedious and ineffective. There were, of course, many other influences, besides this inherent difficulty, which conspired to push prophecy into the background and to bring organisation and system into the foreground. *The Didache*, or Teaching of the Twelve Apostles, written early in the second century, shows prophecy still extant, at least in the rural churches, but it is plainly dying out, and amusing rules are proposed for testing the genuineness of the prophet.

But that former experience of the Spirit in the life of the body and those great outbreaking evidences of it never wholly vanished. The memory and the tradition at least of the outpouring of the Spirit remained as a cherished legacy, and the promise of even " greater things " was not wholly forgotten. Just beyond the middle of the second century there came a sudden revival of prophecy and a fresh consciousness of the immediate presence of the Spirit.

This movement, known in history as Montanism, had many of the characteristics of a primitive emotional revival.[1] The converts called themselves

---

[1] The best early sources for a study of the Montanists are: Eusebius' *Church History*, in which there are many accounts and references; *The*

"pneumatics," and they showed pronounced "orgiastic" traits. The movement was inaugurated by Montanus, a native of Ardabau, in Mysia, not very far from the city of Philadelphia. He had probably been a devotee of the worship of Cybele and had become a Christian somewhere near the middle of the second century. It was about A.D. 157 when he began to "prophesy," and to call the Christians of Phrygia to enter upon a new stage of Christian experience. At first the movement was distinctly rural in type, and it is probable that the old order of "spiritual gifts" had not entirely vanished in those regions. Montanus introduced a fresh burst of emotionalism, and he exalted the importance of ecstasy. He himself was psychically disposed to ecstasy. He believed himself to be a passive instrument of the divine Spirit, and he was convinced that the messages given through him were the *ipsissima verba* of the Deity. "I am the lyre," he said, "and the Spirit is the plectrum that strikes the strings." In other words, he did not claim to be *inspired* but rather to receive divine *dictation*. In this particular, and in the stress laid upon the state of trance, or ecstasy, the type of prophecy was unlike that which is in evidence in the New Testament, and there was good ground for calling it, as the Montanists did do, "new prophecy." Montanus was soon assisted by

41st *Letter of St. Jerome;* and the works, especially the later works, of Tertullian. Of modern studies, the best are Bonwetsch's *Montanismus*, Harnack's *Hist. of Dogma*, Kidd's *A Hist. of the Church*, Vol. I., and Swete's *The Holy Spirit in the Ancient Church*.

HERESIES CONCERNING THE SPIRIT

two women, Prisca and Maximilla, who exhibited the same general type of ecstatic ministry. They gathered a considerable following, and the contagious quality of the revival gave momentum and volume to it. They claimed that there had been an unbroken succession of " prophets " in the Church, but that now a new stage, a stage of maturity, had come. Henceforth the Church was to be guided by *inspired* men and women—pneumatics—rather than by ordained bishops. The Church was to become a congregation of saints instead of a mixed body of pure and impure together. The new stage was, they believed, to be a fulfilment of the promise of Christ—" Greater things than these shall ye do " (John xiv. 12), and " I have many things to say unto you, but ye cannot bear them now " (John xvi. 12). They fired their converts with a heightened zeal for a rigorous and self-denying life. They were ready for the hardest tests of endurance, fasts of a severer type than had previously been practised in the Church, and they gloried in perils even to martyrdom. They insisted that all Church members should live as pure lives as were expected of priests or bishops, and, in accordance with existing practice for priests at that time, they refused to allow second marriages for those Christians who had lost their marital companion by death. They proposed to stem the tide of secularisation which was carrying Christianity into compromise with the world, and they resolved to put an end to double standard morality and to double standard life. They inclined toward a Christianity based upon experience, the testimony of consciousness, rather than upon dogmas or system.

In the strict sense of the word they were not "heretics." They did not positively break with the established *beliefs* of the Church. Some of them inclined to Modalism, but for the most part they had no controversy with accepted doctrine. Their innovations had to do with the *way of life* of Christian believers and with the manner, method and temporal period of divine revelation. They introduced, or possibly revived, a different atmosphere and outlook, a new emotional tone and a "corybantic" fervour. Besides the moral and emotional features they brought in other novelties. They were intense in their apocalyptic expectations. It has been pointed out by W. M. Calder, in a *Bulletin of the John Rylands Library* (for August, 1923), that the Montanist movement was influenced by the description of the descent of the New Jerusalem in the message to the Church of Philadelphia to be found in Revelation iii. 7–13. As we have seen, Philadelphia was near to Ardabau, and a vivid phrase like this apocalyptic one: "The city of my God, the new Jerusalem, *which cometh down out of heaven from my God,*" may very well have fired the imagination of these emotionally-strung zealots. In any case they formed the belief that the New Jerusalem was soon to "come down out of heaven," and they were to be in it and

HERESIES CONCERNING THE SPIRIT

of it when it should come. They chose the near-by town of Pepuza as the spot where the great consummation was to be realised, and around this region, in a high state of glow and fervour, the first stage of Montanism was enacted.

There was a second wave of the movement a few years later in Italy, Gaul and Spain. It did not become in the West the same type of intense and contagious revival as in Asia Minor, nor did it threaten to become to the same degree a menace to the settled order of the Church. At first the Pope saw no danger in the movement and rather welcomed the attempt to raise the tone and fervour of Christian life. Those who were eager for a stricter life and those who wished to emphasise the importance of individual experience and inspiration were drawn to it. The martyrs of Lyons and Vienne were apparently in sympathy with its spirit and life, though there is no evidence that they were actual converts to "the new prophecy." At a later stage, however, when the definite lines of the new movement became better known, and when the authorities of the Church came to realise the full scope and significance of the return to prophecy, they unhesitatingly condemned it and set to work to eradicate it. There was no room in the same Church for authoritative bishops on the one hand and for " pneumatic " prophets, claiming plenary inspiration, on the other !

A third and still more significant wave of Montanism swept over North Africa, and here important

THE CHURCH'S DEBT TO HERETICS

converts were made who gave the movement a new power and a greater dignity. The famous martyrs at Carthage under the persecution of Septimus Severus, Perpetua and Felicitas, were converts to the ' new way," and noble witnesses indeed they proved to be. But the greatest accession to the religion of the Spirit was the famous Carthaginian lawyer, Tertullian, who joined the movement almost as soon as he became acquainted with its aims, probably about 203. Tertullian was naturally a puritan; he had, furthermore, been deeply distressed by the worldliness and compromising spirit everywhere apparent in the Church, so that the rigour and depth of intensity in the new movement made a strong appeal to his sensitive spirit. The marks of fresh vitality, the indications that the Spirit had come in new measure and power, deeply impressed him. He brought great gifts to the new cause, and he gave the movement its only important literary interpretation. A number of his Montanist writings have survived, but a few of them, including his precious treatise on *Ecstasy*, are lost. One of the most valuable extant documents is "*The Passion of the Martyrs, Perpetua and Felicitas.*" In its final editorial form it has often been attributed to Tertullian, though many scholars dissent from that view.

Tertullian's Montanist writings are in a high degree anti-worldly. He takes the ground that a Christian cannot fight, *i.e.*, cannot be a soldier,[1] nor,

---
[1] See *De corona militis*.

HERESIES CONCERNING THE SPIRIT

indeed, be contaminated by the idolatry involved in art, trade and public life,[1] and of course he is uncompromisingly opposed to the shows and games in the theatre and arena.[2] He carries his asceticism to irrational limits, and he is passionately eager for martyrdom. In his accounts of prophecy and ecstasy he is more restrained than the early Phrygian Montanists were. He believes strongly, however, in the immediate work of the Holy Spirit and in continuous revelation. In fact, Tertullian bears an unmistakable testimony in favour of progress and development under the guidance of the Spirit. The great "epoch" is in the future, not in the past. "The Lord sent the Paraclete," he wrote, "since human imperfection could not receive everything at once, and so that the disciples of life might step by step be guided and ordered and brought to perfection by His Vicar, the Holy Spirit. 'I have still many things to say to you,' He said, 'but ye cannot bear them now. When the Spirit of Truth is come, He shall guide you into all the Truth.' What, then, does the dispensation of the Spirit mean but disciplinary guidance, the remoulding of the mind and an advance to *better things*? Nothing is without stages of growth; all things have their times and seasons."[3] He concludes, then, that "the stage of final maturity" is the dispensation of the Spirit which has now at length begun.[4]

---

[1] See *De idololatria*.
[2] See *De spectaculis*, perhaps written in the ante-Montanist period.
[3] *De monogamia*, I.
[4] *Ibid.*, I.

THE CHURCH'S DEBT TO HERETICS

Tertullian does not admit the charge made by the Church that Montanist " prophecy " is something new ; it is, he holds, only the completion and perfection of early prophecy and revelation. The Holy Spirit, he declares, brings nothing new ; He clearly reveals and brings to remembrance what has before been intimated and hinted. He is the restorer and completer rather than the originator.[1] Tertullian did much to bring forcibly home to Christian consciousness the dangers that lurk in ecclesiasticism and institutionalism, and he, more than any one else, sounded the alarm against worldliness and laxity. The remedy for all these ills is the fresh, full life in the Spirit.

Unfortunately the Montanists were too prone to take artificial short cuts, or to run off into vague enthusiasms. They inclined, too, to set up the " revelations," which had come through their " prophets," as a new and higher " law," superior even to the New Testament, and they vainly hoped to head off worldliness by establishing puritanic regulations. They rendered, however, a real service to the great faith of the ages by emphasising once more the vital fact of the divine presence in the world, the truth of continuous revelation, and the immense significance of the Spirit in the life of the Church. They called the Church back to the original sources of life and inspiration, and they protested against the deadness of officialism and " authority." They

[1] *De monogamia*, II.

HERESIES CONCERNING THE SPIRIT

rightly set the inspired leader above the office-holder. The time was not ripe for the ideal Church, nor were they wise and sane enough to build an ideal spiritual Church, but they at least revealed that the existing one was not ideal. They set a movement going which was never to stop—a subtle influence that was destined to be endlessly contagious.

The most immediate and striking result of Montanism was its effect upon the final formation of the New Testament canon. The Church met the proclamation of a new era of prophecy with the authoritative declaration that revelation was closed and prophecy was at an end. It was not an accident that the last chapter of the last book in the canon said: " I testify unto every man that heareth the words of the prophecy of this book, if any man shall add unto them, God shall add unto him the plagues that are written in this book " (Rev. xxii. 18). Henceforth it becomes *perilous* for any person claiming the inspiration of the Spirit to give forth authoritative disclosures or instructions or messages. The channel of truth is not to be the lonely individual in communion with God, but the supernaturally ordained hierarchy of the Church.

With severity and ruthlessness these simple witnesses to the Spirit were gradually annihilated or suppressed. The Emperor Justinian found that there were still some of these poor heretics surviving in his reign, but they were finally " eliminated " by methods of force and brutality, and one hopes that

THE CHURCH'S DEBT TO HERETICS

the devoted souls found at last the New Jerusalem which failed to come down from heaven when they expected it. But, as a matter of fact, believers in the continuous presence of the Spirit were really never altogether eliminated. The separate organisation of Montanists ceased to exist, and claims of inspiration were hushed. But the *faith* never wholly died out of the world. It was driven out of sight and became a submerged stream, but its warm waters never ceased to flow. Later outbreaks, or revivals, reveal similar traits, and use corresponding symbols. The lily, or lily-twig, which was the Montanist flower-symbol for the epoch of the Spirit, succeeding the nettle and the thorny rose of the two earlier dispensations, was again and again revived by the little groups, who in their turn were " looking for the consolation of Israel."

The great mystics found a way to experience a relation with God without falling into heresy. The writings which were attributed to Dionysius, St. Paul's convert on Mars Hill, but which were actually written by a Neo-Platonist Christian at the close of the fifth century, or at the beginning of the sixth, came, in the course of time, to form one of the most important strands of mystical influence. But St. Augustine had already introduced a form of mysticism—drawn also from Neo-Platonism—which harmonised with his Roman Catholic type of Christianity. The three greatest early interpreters of Western mysticism, St. Augustine, St. Gregory the

HERESIES CONCERNING THE SPIRIT

Great and St. Bernard of Clairvaux, succeeded in formulating a method of mystical experience which was not "orgiastic," enthusiastic, charismatic, but rather a normal, rational procedure, and a feature of genuine spiritual life when brought into union with divine Grace. These great geniuses worked out a mystical theology and a method of contemplation that were neither explosive nor revolutionary, that heightened the spiritual quality of life without entailing any grave dangers to peace or sanity.

John Scotus Erigena, in the ninth century, set forth a pantheistical conception of God and man which held seed thoughts that were both explosive and revolutionary. He represents a strong anti-Augustinian strand of thought which was henceforth to come into rivalry with the system of the Carthaginian saint, and was, whenever it emerged, to be a source of disturbance and a spring of heresy. Erigena was the foremost scholar of that century in Europe, and he was called from his native retreat in Ireland to be the founder of the famous Palatine School in Paris, out of which the University of Paris was later born. He translated the Greek writings of pseudo-Dionysius into Latin, and so made them current coin for the coming centuries, and he also wrote an extraordinary book, *On the Division of Nature*, which introduced into Christian channels a philosophy of God, of the world, of man, and of the divine-human relationship, that did not fit very well into the safe schemes of theology. He revived the

THE CHURCH'S DEBT TO HERETICS

Montanist idea of progressive revelation. For him the true Church is the invisible Church, the Church of the Spirit. The one important form of communion, he held, takes place where spirit meets with Spirit, and there is an unending procession of God who continually unveils Himself in saintly souls. This Irish John was suspected of heresy in his lifetime, particularly in his views on the sacrament, and those who took the pains to read him in the two centuries after his death were puzzled over his unusual views, but there were no " contaminating " effects apparent during this period. In the first years of the thirteenth century, however, there suddenly emerged in Paris a movement which can be traced directly to the influence of his writings, and which seemed to the Church officials to be fraught with grave danger to " sound religion." It was discovered that a celebrated master in the University of Paris was teaching that only those are saved who are joined in living membership with Christ. This was Amaury, often called Amalric, of Bene, who had been studying the writings of John Scotus, and who had come to the conclusion that the reign of God is in the hearts of men, and that salvation is a vital inward process by which man is brought into living union with Christ the Spirit. Amaury had many disciples. He himself held many Montanist ideas, though there is no positive historical connection with a submerged Montanist tradition. Amaury was an ordained man and a scholar of

HERESIES CONCERNING THE SPIRIT

repute. He was probably born near Chartres, though his birth date and place cannot be fixed with certainty. He perhaps owed his "tendency" originally to the influence of the school of Chartres, a school with pantheistic leanings, especially to Bernard of Tours, who was writing his *De mundi universitate* when Amaury was a boy. This school of Chartres was attached to the famous cathedral of the city, and it had a succession of distinguished teachers, among whom William of Conches and Gilbert of La Porrée (who himself was charged with heresy) may be especially mentioned. It was a nursery of free thought and had a heretical bent. The reports concerning Amaury's position are from his prejudiced opponents, and they do scarce justice to his serious view—that something of the Divine is revealed in man, and that "no one can be saved unless he believes himself to be a living member of Christ." Amaury further "spiritualised" heaven and hell as inner states rather than as places. Those who are ignorant of the truth are in hell, and those who know the truth are in paradise now. The true nature of religion is a life in the Spirit ; when that is attained sacraments become unimportant.[1] Humanity has had a stage of discipline under the law ; it was later regenerated by Grace, and now it is being revivified by the breath of the Holy Spirit

---

[1] Hauréau, *Hist. Phil. Scol.*, Part II., Vol. I., Chap. 5, gives the substance of a contemporary document which he discovered in the Library of Troyes.

into a life of purity. This final transformation is taking place; already certain privileged souls are in possession of the Spirit who inspires and guides them. Among those who have this experience *knowledge* has taken the place of *faith*, and *confidence* of *hope*. John Scotus Erigena was plainly considered the source of these " errors," for his writings were officially condemned by Pope Honorius III., January 25th, 1225, and the disciples of Amaury were linked up with the condemnation.

Amaury himself died in 1205, soon after his condemnation, first by the authorities of the University and later by the Pope, but his followers formed a Society, the members of which claimed that the actual reign of the Holy Spirit in the hearts of men had begun. The little group met in some obscure place in Paris, where they practised silent worship, and where they listened to the spontaneous prayers and messages of their " prophets." They maintained that there had been successive dispensations, but that now the Holy Spirit had come to incarnate Himself in men, and was bringing to an end the period of law, commandments and sacraments. The mature and final stage of divine revelation, they claimed, is the revelation of the Spirit in the lives of men. The little band was " surprised," their leaders captured, many put to death by fire, and others banished.[1] The attempts to stamp out this movement only spread it more widely. Disciples or followers of

[1] For fuller details, see my *Studies in Mystical Religion*, Chap. X.

HERESIES CONCERNING THE SPIRIT

Amaury were discovered in fairly large numbers in the dioceses of Sens, Langres and Troyes. The next " outbreak " of a similar revival appeared in Strasbourg, where a " prophet," named Ortlieb, formed a group of followers similar to the " Amaurians " in Paris. He discarded all externals and claimed to have " the leading of the Holy Spirit." There came to light in the following period a large number of similar societies, variously named by the Church inquisitors " Brethren of the free Spirit," or " the sect of the new Spirit," but all exhibiting traits similar to the Montanists, and all expressing a set purpose to break utterly with the historic Church. More restrained and more strictly organised mystical groups were formed, under the name of Beghards for the men and Beguines for the women. They partook of the general " spiritual " movement of the time, the penchant for poverty, and the life of " undisciplined vagrancy." This very widespread revival of enthusiasm, and of faith in the guidance of the Spirit, may possibly have, and probably does have, some hidden and subterranean connection with another curious movement which had its origin a little before the discovery of the Amaurians was made—I mean the spiritual movement inaugurated by Joachim da Fiori, and which led on into " the Eternal Gospel " and " the spiritual Franciscans."

Joachim da Fiori was born at Celico, near Cosenza, in the province of Calabria, Italy, in 1131. There is much evidence that Joachim was under the in-

THE CHURCH'S DEBT TO HERETICS

fluence of Greek Christianity; in fact, it has been pointed out that Calabria was at this time half Greek, and held many views in common with the Cathari.[1] He was of bourgeois origin, though his family held high positions. He received a good education for the time and became a page in a ducal court of the region. His deepest interest, however, centred in the Holy Land, especially Jerusalem, of which he heard pilgrims and Crusaders tell their fascinating tales. He lived in the period of Arnold of Brescia and Frederick Barbarossa. Finally " this youth of angelic countenance " went himself to see the land of his dreams. While he was in Constantinople there raged a terrible pestilence, and death stalked everywhere. He sent back his escort and attendants, and with a single companion went on afoot as a devout pilgrim. There is a well-known legend which tells how, almost dying of thirst in the desert, Joachim had a vision of a man standing by a river of oil and saying to him, "Drink of this stream." When he woke he saw that *this stream* was the Scriptures, and that now of a sudden he understood their meaning.

He visited Jerusalem, the Holy Sepulchre, and many other scenes of the Bible. Finally on Mount Tabor, which he believed to be the scene of the Transfiguration, he had a vision of Christ and His way of life. He vowed to follow Christ, to give up

[1] See Turberville's *Mediæval Heresy and the Inquisition* (London, 1920), p. 34.

HERESIES CONCERNING THE SPIRIT

the glory of the court, and become a herald of the Cross and of the message of the Gospels. He had a great mystical experience on the night of the Resurrection, a splendour broke around him and at the same time he was inwardly filled with divine light, and then he saw the complete accord of Old and New Testaments. On his return he entered the Cistercian monastery at Sambucina, where he acted as humble porter and where he studied the Scriptures and prepared to fulfil his vision. At length he left the brotherhood and went out as a lay preacher, speaking in the vulgar tongue, announcing the coming of a new age. He became an itinerant preacher of righteousness and of the necessity for radical change of life as preparation for the Kingdom of God, near at hand. But a layman was not allowed to preach, and after running the hazard for some years Joachim decided to enter a Cistercian monastery at Corazzo in 1168, where he was ordained and where he gave himself once more to meditation and study.

After ten years of life as a pure aspirant and mystic he was chosen Abbot and plunged into the tangle of affairs much against his will. On the news of his election he fled, but was brought back. He secured a release from the Pope (1181) and left his disagreeable duties as Abbot to go into an undisturbed hermit life as "a solitary," praying, having ecstasies and preparing his prophetic message of the new age, when the Holy Spirit would hold complete sway. He gained the reputation of a saint, living an austere life and, at the same time, a life full of good and holy deeds. An early chronicler says that " he had learned from Christ to be gentle and humble of heart," and Gebhart adds, " His simplicity and charity were admirable : he warmed on his bosom the heads of the dying. In the winter that preceded his death, when famine was raging in Calabria and Sicily, he gave his last garments to the poor ; he washed with his own hands the floor of the infirmary ; he saved the towns from the ferocious brutality of Henry VI.; he bent over every bed of suffering without troubling about the sufferer's religion."[1] The people flocked to him, and many tried to join with him. He only moved farther on and higher up, " amid the very cold Alps," and finally established himself in a hermitage at Fiori, consecrated to St. John the Forerunner, and here, in this quiet retreat, he founded a stricter branch of the Cistercian Order, and became Abbot of the monastery which he founded.

In 1196, the Pope, Celestine III., approved of the congregation of hermits in the new abbey and the Order of stricter monks which had gathered around Joachim, who gave much of his time to writing and left several works behind him. He died in 1202. Two years before his death he submitted all his writings to the Pope for examination, but he died before judgment was passed. He impressed his own generation with his power as a prophet. He himself

[1] Gebhart, *Mystics and Heretics in Italy at the End of the Middle Ages*, p. 84.

HERESIES CONCERNING THE SPIRIT

believed absolutely in his own revelations, and he sincerely thought himself to be an organ of revelation. He was, however, restrained in his prophecies, and was content to proclaim the decline of the Church, the impure character of the clergy, and to predict, in general terms, the near end of the old *régime* and the coming of a new world. His followers and other enthusiasts in his name produced a large quantity of prophetic literature, and they loaded their books with exact predictions which they attributed to the Abbot of Fiori. His name came to be a venerated one and almost a synonym for " prophet." He was believed almost universally to have received supernatural guidance and special divine assistance. He lived and worked, as Renan says, surrounded *d'une auréole de mystère*. He saw the general condition of Christianity, as the same writer declares, " with rare clairvoyance."[1] Dante refers to him as one " endowed with the prophetic spirit."[2]

It was this " prophet " of Fiori who first promulgated " the Eternal Gospel." The written word, he held, is a dead letter—it cannot serve for the completion of the life of the Church. Only a gospel filled with the Holy Spirit can do this work. In the Apocalypse he found much of his material, and here he found his phrase—the Eternal Gospel, *i.e.*, the gospel that is ever living, in place of the letter that kills. The Church with its secular entanglements is

[1] Renan, *Nouvelles Études*, p. 221.
[2] *Paradiso*, XII. 140.

THE CHURCH'S DEBT TO HERETICS

only a tent to be removed and to give place to the permanent spiritual House which God is to set up. He also taught that there are three ages or dispensations, that of the Father, that of the Son, and that of the Holy Ghost. The Church is Hagar in the wilderness, the new Church under the Holy Spirit will be Sarah the beloved. Once more we have the stage of nettles and roses which is to be followed by the blossoming of the lily. By far-fetched symbolism and inferences Joachim named the year 1260 as the date when the old order would end and the new begin. He dreamed of a purified and spiritual Christianity which would succeed and replace the legal, literal and external type, but he missed the true path to a spiritual world, and forecast a world of monks and saints living a cloistered life, a Christianity culminating in visions and contemplation.

After a period of seeming slumber, which was really a period of gestation, the message of "the Eternal Gospel" suddenly burst forth with new significance in 1254, six years before the date which Joachim set for the *new epoch*. Much had happened in between. Francis of Assisi had come with his inspiration, and had worked his miracle of love and poverty. He had gone and had left behind him three brotherhood Orders, the most important of which historically was the Order of the Brothers Minor, the Franciscan Friars. This Order, even before Francis's death in 1226, and still more decidedly after it, showed two marked tendencies, one toward a loose

HERESIES CONCERNING THE SPIRIT

interpretation of the ideal of Francis and the other toward a strict and rigorous interpretation of it—tendencies which have, of course, marked the whole of Christian history. One part of the Order soon showed itself incapable of rising to the superhuman venture. This majority party undertook to adjust the Rule of Francis to fit the possibilities of human nature. The other party held with startling audacity that the mission of their saint was not finished yet, that this mission was above everything else in the world, even above the Pope and the Church, and involved the fulfilment of the revelation and purpose of God. This party, which later came to be designated as " the Spirituals " or " Spiritual Franciscans," came strongly under the influence of the writings of Joachim, knowing no distinction between those writings that were genuine and those that were spurious, of which latter class there was a long list. These Franciscans were mystical and intense. They were disillusioned regarding the Church and no less so towards the secularised Order of Friars. They were alike impressed by the power of Francis's spiritual experiment, and by the Calabrian's prophecy that a new spiritual Order would arise to inaugurate the coming era.

It was the intense and enthusiastic group of " spirituals," gathered around John of Parma, who was General of the Order from 1247 to 1257, out of which the famous " Eternal Gospel " emerged. It was produced under the inspiration of Joachim, but it was matured as a project to restore the glory and power of St. Francis's Order. The author of it was Gerard of Borgo San Donnino, a learned man, a pure spirit, "temperate, modest, amiable ; in a word, a most admirable and lovable character."[1] John of Parma was almost certainly in sympathy with the author in his literary venture. Gerard's book consisted of an Introduction, together with Joachim's three treatises in shortened form, the combined work making up "the Eternal Gospel."[2] The Introduction declared that the spiritual meaning of Scripture has not been entrusted to the Pope. "He has received commission only to interpret the literal sense of it. If he takes upon himself to give the spiritual meaning his judgment is rash, and no one need pay attention to it. Spiritual persons are not bound to obey the Roman Church nor to acquiesce in its judgment on spiritual matters." The Introduction further declared that "the gospel of Christ was not the real gospel of the kingdom. It did not build the true Church. It did not bring any one to perfection. The reign of God is inaugurated by the Eternal Gospel which is about to be preached to all nations. The messengers of this new gospel are superior even to those of the primitive Church."[3]

---

[1] Lea, *History of the Inquisition*, Vol. III., p. 24.
[2] Gerard's *Liber introductorius in Evangelium aeternum* is preserved in fragmentary form in the Bibliothèque Nationale (Sorbonne Collections, Nos. 1726, XIV. siècle, fol. 38, V., and fol. 48).
[3] These quotations are translated from Renan, *Nouvelles Études*, pp. 286, 289.

HERESIES CONCERNING THE SPIRIT

The Introduction was thus an exaggeration of Joachim's prophecies. It set forth the beginning of an era of the Spirit which was to be a complete break with the existing Church. It was the culmination of the " spiritual " aspirations of the period. Gerard's book was condemned to be burnt, and the author was banished to a monastery. His fall carried down with him John of Parma, who was demoted from his generalship in 1257 at Ara Cœli and was sent to a retreat in a monastery near Rieti, though his sentence was softened and he was gradually restored to favour.[1] Brother Giles was right in his forecast at the time of John's election, when he said : " Thou hast come fortunately and opportunely, brother, *but thou hast come late.*" For thirty-two years in his retreat John " lived the life of an angel." He became the friend of Popes and gained a wide sphere of spiritual influence. " I could give wholesome counsel," he once said, " if there were any one to listen to me, but in the Roman courts little is discussed but wars and triumphs, not the salvation of souls."[2]

Bonaventura succeeded John of Parma as General of the Order, and he led a reaction against the mission and the campaign of " the spirituals." He, though a mystic himself and opposed to the worldliness of

---

[1] The documentary account of the Commission which passed upon the Eternal Gospel at Anagni, and condemned the Introduction and its author, is given with the Protocol by Father Denifle, in *Archiv für Litt. und Kirchen-Geschichte*, Vol. I., pp. 49–142.

[2] Lea, *Hist. of Inqui.*, Vol. III., p. 25.

THE CHURCH'S DEBT TO HERETICS

the Church, was determined to keep the Order "safe and sound" and in harmony with the Church. Bonaventura was chosen in 1260 to write the life of Francis, and three years later his work was officially approved by the general chapter as the standard life of Francis to the exclusion of all existing "legends." This was a plan for the exclusion of the dangerous "tendencies" afloat. The Church, under Gregory IX., had calmly decided to subordinate the Order rigidly to the Church, and the work of Bonaventura marks a new stage in this stern process. The overwhelming difficulties attending the realisation of Francis's ideals, and the dreams of his holy brotherhood, drove many of the "brothers" to take refuge in the visions of Joachim and to push these hopes to extremes, especially under the spur of persecution. A little group of spiritual leaders, Peter John Olivi, in Provence, and Ubertino of Casale, Angelo Clareno,[1] and Brother Liberato of Italy, came strongly under the influence of Joachim's writings and the later additions. They were intensely devoted to his life of purity and poverty, but they were hated by the Church officials and the Order. One of the inquisitors said to Liberato : "Never was meat sold dearer in a butcher's shop than the price your flesh would bring."[2]

Ubertino of Casale was the leader of the Tuscan

---

[1] Angelo Clareno also wrote a Franciscan Chronicle. His sympathies were with "the spirituals."
[2] D. S. Muzzey, *Spiritual Franciscans*, p. 9.

HERESIES CONCERNING THE SPIRIT

" Spirituals." He was shocked at the " fall " of the Brothers from the ideals of St. Francis. He declared that many of them have wealth and full cellars, and that they live like other Christians ! He devoted himself to the task of gathering a pure flock of God in Tuscany, though they were eventually forced to seek refuge in Sicily.

Angelo Clareno and Liberato were condemned to perpetual imprisonment in 1274, but they were taken from prison and sent by Raymond Gaufride, who was in sympathy with them, on a mission to the heretics of Armenia. They returned safely after many experiences of perils of travel and perils among false brethren. When they sought a quiet retreat in the Mark of Ancona, in their home province, one of the vicars of the region declared that he would " rather receive and shelter a band of fornicators in his province than these two men." These Spirituals of the " Marches " were originators of the *Fraticelli*. Angelo, writing in 1317, when Pope John XXII. was proceeding to exterminate this heresy, wrote : " Truth triumphs over all and is immovable. We do not consider ourselves either apostates or heretics, since it cannot be a heresy to confess what St. Francis himself believed."[1] Clareno was during his life considered head of the strict Brothers, and in one of his letters to them he said : " Christ speaks to us at sundry times and in divers manners, by the Fathers, the Apostles, the Prophets and the Martyrs,

[1] Bonet-Maury, *Précurseurs*, p. 129.

THE CHURCH'S DEBT TO HERETICS

but in these last times He has spoken to us by His seraphic son St. Francis, whom He designed to be the inheritor of all the witnesses. Jesus Christ called Francis to the practice of perfect poverty; He ordered him to adopt the evangelical rule—the rule of the Gospel. To seek heavenly things and to despise earthly things, to hold to those things which are before, that is our vow, the pledge of our immortality. What if a king or a pope orders us to do something contrary to this faith, to this love, to these works, we shall obey God rather than men. Christ our only Saviour teaches us all, by the example of His life and His Divine preachings, the path of salvation and righteousness." [1]

Celestine V., who was chosen Pope in 1294, as a compromise to unite the rival factions, the Colonnas and the Orsini, was in spiritual sympathy with the " Spirituals." He commended their purpose to live strictly and to obey the rule of poverty. He absolved them from all obedience to the authorities of the Order, and named them " Poor Hermits of Celestine," with Liberato as their leader. He made " the great refusal " before he had ruled a year, and all his acts were later declared null, and under his successor, Boniface VIII., " the Spirituals " were once more severely dealt with. Boniface issued a letter of condemnation against them, and under John XXII. they were classed with many other types of heretics, and sweepingly condemned, but

[1] Bonet-Maury, *Précurseurs*, p. 130.

HERESIES CONCERNING THE SPIRIT

they existed in quite large numbers until the Reformation.

After the early period—the fine and beautiful period—of the history of "the Spirituals" they belong with "the anti-clerical groups," which will be dealt with in a later chapter, rather than with "the heretics of the Spirit." The thirteenth and fourteenth centuries reveal such a *mélange* of "heresies" that it is almost impossible to classify them. They interlock and fuse together, and the next two chapters will deal with movements which partly belong with the groups I have been studying here.

These champions of the Spirit from the days of Montanus to the days of Joachim were often wild and confused. They were enthusiasts, "pneumatics," and they often took a "rebel" attitude toward existing institutions and systems. They belong in the "dangerous" line of mystical descent, through the Irish philosopher, John Scotus Erigena, rather than in the "safe" line through St. Augustine and Bernard of Clairvaux. The same two lines of danger and safety appear again at the Reformation. But these men whom I have here reviewed were real light-bearers and contributors, and we owe some of our greatest privileges of freedom and spiritual autonomy to their championship, their sufferings and their brave witness in the fires of martyrdom.

CHAPTER VII

THE BACKGROUND AND ENVIRONMENT OF ANTI-CHURCH HERESIES AND SCHISMS

THE first Christians of the Jerusalem group felt, at least from the time of Pentecost, that they formed the true Israel within Israel—the chosen Remnant, or Seed of God. They began at once to use the ancient Greek word *ecclesia* to name their fellowship, and the word, as well as the body named by it, was destined to have a remarkable history. St. Paul used the same famous name for his Gentile congregations, and he showed throughout his apostolic period a great concern for the " edification " of the body, the *ecclesia*, the Church, and no less for its unity. The divisions which threatened its unity and its life always grieved his spirit and caused him deep suffering. It was " carnal-mindedness," he maintained, and not " spiritual-mindedness," that led the Church at Corinth to divide into rival parties, each one saying, " I am of Paul, or I am of Apollos, or I am of Cephas, or I am of Christ." " Is Christ divided ? " the Apostle asks. In his later correspondence he stresses even more than in his earlier Epistles the importance of unity, oneness, unbroken fellowship. " There is one body, and one Spirit, even as also ye are called in one hope of your calling;

ANTI-CHURCH HERESIES AND SCHISMS

one Lord, one faith, one baptism, one God and Father of all, who is over all, and through all, and in all" (Eph. iv. 4–6). The whole Church, he declared, " grows into a Holy Temple in the Lord ; in whom ye also are builded together for a habitation of God in the Spirit " (Eph. ii. 21–22). All walls of partition are to be broken down, all enmity to be abolished, and peace and reconciliation are at length to prevail.

But unity proved to be a difficult and elusive ideal. St. Paul took his adventurous last journey to Jerusalem in the hope that he might possibly, through the influence of the great Gentile collection, draw the two wings—the Jewish and Gentile wings —of the primitive Church together, but he found the opposition in Jerusalem too great to be overcome and he died with the great reconciliation unaccomplished.

The successors to the first Apostles passed their entire lives in an unbroken struggle with heresies and divisions. The writers of the latest New Testament books are face to face with these stern issues, and so, too, in like manner, are Polycarp and Ignatius and Irenæus. In fact, some of the main types of early Christian literature are treatises against heretics. One of the early Greek philosophers, Empedocles, held that " love " and " strife," *i.e.*, cohesion and repulsion, were the two elemental building forces of the universe, and they both seem to have continued to operate among the

THE CHURCH'S DEBT TO HERETICS

early Christians. Love and cohesion drew the *ecclesia* together, but strife and repulsion, which St. Paul called " fruits of the flesh," were also always in evidence within its domain. The Donatists came into existence after the turmoil of persecution under Diocletian (284–305) without in the first instance having any well-matured opposition to the Church as an institution. The first leaders of the movement were simply determined to resist what seemed to them the secularisation of the Church and the encroachment of the State. They took an attitude of rigour and proposed to stand for a Church separate from the world and untainted by its corruptions. The issue was raised at first as a practical result of persecution. Many of the Christian officials had failed to stand the severe tests of the persecution. They had saved their lives by an evasive compromise. The persecutors had demanded the officials of the Churches, generally the bishops, to deliver up the sacred writings of the Church. If they refused they were tortured, mutilated, or even killed, while if they yielded, and became *traditors*, they escaped suffering and death. There were many who took the easy way out, and the strict, or puritan, party set itself against the *traditors* and their way of compromise. They themselves glorified martyrdom, and they claimed that the real Church should be winnowed clean of the worldly chaff and should be composed only of those who could stand to the uttermost the fiery tests of persecution.

ANTI-CHURCH HERESIES AND SCHISMS

The controversy came to a head over the consecration of a bishop to succeed Mensurius, Bishop of Carthage, who died in 311. Cæcilian, archdeacon under Mensurius, was chosen bishop and was consecrated by Felix, Bishop of Aptunga. A powerful opposition at once developed against the recognition of Cæcilian as bishop. The opposition sprang out of a great variety of motives, and was by no means pure and unmixed zeal for truth and holiness. Nevertheless, there was in the movement of opposition an honest *basis* of zeal for a Church uncompromised by surrender to worldly force and influence. A party formed against Cæcilian, and one of their counts against him was that he had been consecrated by a *traditor* bishop whose act for that reason, they claimed, was invalid. They proceeded to declare the see of Carthage vacant, and they elected Majorinus bishop and had him consecrated. Majorinus died about 315, and was succeeded by Donatus, often called Donatus the Great, though he preferred to be called Donatus of Carthage. It was from him that the party eventually took its name.[1] He was a man of vigour, learning, ability and unimpeachable life.

There were other similar controversies over the consecration of bishops and many of the struggles were petty and bitterly partisan, but gradually, as the lines of the movement differentiated, the Dona-

[1] There was another Donatus, usually known as Donatus of Casæ Nigræ—Black Hut—who supported Majorinus.

tists came to stand for the puritan ideal of a spiritual Church led by spiritual men. They took the ground that religious services cease to be valid if the officiating priest or bishop is living a life of sin and is spiritually unqualified to perform spiritual functions. The measure of power of a Church, they claimed, is to be found, not in wealth or splendour, not in the number, or the social standing of the membership, but in the purity of life and the holiness of the members, especially of the ordained. They were shocked by the paganising of the Church under Constantine, by the inrush of half-Christians, and by the lowered level of faith and practice. Quite inconsistently, however, they manœuvred in the early period to secure the secular support of Constantine, and they did many other things which compromised their high profession, but, on the whole, they stood for a purified Church and a ministry exercised by clean and holy men. One of the most important of the distinctions which they made was their emphasis on the inner spirit, the *subjective* side of religion as against the prevailing emphasis on the *objective* side. It was generally assumed in " the great Church" that ordination imparted to a priest a certain objective quality which made all his sacramental and sacerdotal acts efficacious regardless of the moral and spiritual state of his own life. This objective theory made it less urgent and necessary for the ordained person to be scrupulously pure, uncompromisingly holy and unspotted by the world. In any case his

ANTI-CHURCH HERESIES AND SCHISMS

ministerial acts would accomplish their purpose, precisely as a scientific doctor's prescriptions would do, whatever might be the moral character of either.

It was against this theory of magical *objective effects* that the best of the Donatists bore their testimony and fought their fight. They protested against conferring upon an institution qualities which could properly belong only to persons. Instead of pronouncing the Church to be " holy," they stood for real holiness of life in those who composed the Church. Instead of calling the sacrament " holy " they wanted the officiators of it and the partakers of it to be pure and righteous. But the final victory of the Church over the Donatists tended strongly to establish the Church as the one divine institution and as the mysterious instrument of Grace and salvation. The " holiness " of the Church came to be considered superior to, and independent of, the holiness of character in the lives of the membership of the Church, and it was thought of as an *entity* above and beyond the visible Church, with a magical efficacy all its own. To the struggle for victory over the Donatists St. Augustine gave his powerful mind and pen, and the controversy carried him to a position the extreme opposite of that held by the Donatists. In his book *On Baptism*, and in his treatise *On the Correction of the Donatists*, he raised the objective theory of the Church to its apex, and made this institution the most divine and august entity in the world. There can be, he maintained, only one

THE CHURCH'S DEBT TO HERETICS

Church, the authoritative *ecclesia* which Christ came to the earth to establish. Its authority rests upon an uninterrupted succession of bishops, ordained originally by the Apostles themselves, who, in turn, were ordained by Christ. The sacraments of the Church belong solely to this mysterious institution, and they are, in this world of sin and evil, the extraordinary channels of divine Grace. They are efficacious through the miraculous power bestowed upon the priestly celebrant by his ordination, and they *work* independently of the moral character of the priest or the subjective disposition of the recipient. They are effective even in the case of infants who receive them unconsciously. They are " holy " channels of Grace. But outside the Church there is no salvation. No one can have God for Father unless he has the Church for his Mother. No one can have Grace unless he uses the means of Grace. No one can possess Jesus Christ, the Head of the Church, unless he belongs to Christ's Body, which is the Church. The Donatists were champions of religion as a way of life. They called men back to the Sermon on the Mount. They wanted the personal fruits of the Spirit and not an impersonal institution. The time was not ripe for their ideals, and they were themselves not always true to these ideals, but they were voices crying in the wilderness, and their cry was not altogether in vain. For the next thousand years the ideas which lay at the heart of the Donatist movement were recurrent. The prevailing heresies from

ANTI-CHURCH HERESIES AND SCHISMS

the opening of the twelfth century onward, as we shall see, emphasised the subjective aspect of Christianity as against the objective aspect of it. The notable heretics insisted upon moral and spiritual qualities of life while they opposed the claims of the Church as a mysterious entity and an instrument of Grace.

There was another contemporary movement, which began outside the Church, but which was destined to have immense influence upon the Church itself and even greater influence upon heretical groups that were at a later time arrayed against the Church. This was Manichæism. Its founder was Mani, or Manes, the Latin form of which was Manichæus. His birthplace was in that frontier region which may be called either Persia or Babylonia, and he was born about 216. He experienced many " revelations " and had traits not unlike those which appeared later in Mohammed. He wrote many treatises and he was a talented painter. He gathered disciples about him and began his public mission in Persia sometime before the middle of the century, and he seems to have suffered a brutal martyrdom, probably at the hands of the Zoroastrian priesthood in 277. The early sources for his teaching are very meagre, and most of our information comes from opponents who are hostile, bitter and unfair. St. Augustine is naturally the most celebrated source. He mildly professed the Manichæan faith from 373 to 382. Of their views he always speaks vaguely and in indefinite general terms but with repulsion. In the *Confessions* he says : " I fell among men raving with pride, very carnal and wordy, in whose mouths were the snares of the Devil and a bird lime made up of a mixture of the syllables of Thy name and of our Lord Jesus Christ and of the Holy Ghost, the Paraclete, our Comforter. Because I thought them to be Thee I fed upon them ; not greedily, for Thou didst not in them savour to me as Thou art ; for Thou wast not these empty figments, nor was I nourished by them, but rather exhausted. Upon such empty husks was I then fed : yet was not fed." [1]

The most exact and reliable information comes from Mohammedan sources. The later followers, who lived in Moslem territory, preserved many traditions of the founder and some accounts of the early stages of the movement. One important passage has survived which may very probably be a quotation from the founder himself. " Wisdom and deeds," he says, " have from time to time been brought to mankind by the messengers of God. In one age they have been brought by the messenger called Buddha to India, in another by Zaradusht (Zoroaster) to Persia, in another by Jesus to the West. Thereupon this revelation, this prophecy in the last age, has come down through me, Mani, the messenger of the God of Truth to Babylonia." [2]

[1] *Confessions*, III. 6. Passage not given in full.
[2] This is found in Al-Biruni, a Mohammedan writer, who quotes it from a Manichæan writing. Al-Biruni died in 1048. His *Chronology of Ancient Nations* was translated into English in 1879.

ANTI-CHURCH HERESIES AND SCHISMS

Mani's system is a fusion of ideas from Persian religion, Babylonian folk-lore, Buddhist teaching, Old Testament cosmology, and Christian doctrines. It was deeply coloured by Gnostic features, and thus it fitted the mental outlook of the period and of the lands where it spread. The system maintained a sharp *dualism* between good and evil, light and darkness, though it appears not to have made as much of the evil character of *matter* as the earlier Gnostics did. God is Light and wherever Light is the spiritual forces are triumphant, while, on the other hand, Satan, the primal Devil, is the product of darkness, and is in the ascendancy wherever darkness prevails. God made the world to be ruled by Light and He made the primal Man, who was a spiritual being, but Satan made Adam and Eve, our actual human ancestors, on purpose to undermine and spoil God's plans with the world. Satan, however, used some elements of Light in making these human parents, and this Light element is in man the one ground for human redemption. Man's sensual nature is the result of his dark and evil elements, but there is in him a Light principle by which he may be saved. Jesus was sent to defeat the Devil and to conquer the forces of darkness. The Manichæans were divided into two spiritual grades, the *Hearers*, or ordinary members, and the *Elect*, or spiritual leaders, sometimes called the Perfect. Persons of this second grade lived very strict lives. Under no circumstances did they destroy human life, and, where possible, they avoided taking even animal life. They refrained from using evil words such as oaths. They utterly refused marriage and thought of the propagation of life as a positive evil, since it meant the re-imprisonment of Light substance in a body. The Manichæan Church in Augustine's period appears to have had three orders of officials. Very little knowledge is available about their sacraments, though they probably practised a form of baptism and perhaps a simple sacramental meal. They used the trinitarian terms, Father, Son and Holy Ghost, and there are some indications that Mani believed himself to be an incarnation of the Paraclete, though it is more likely that he called himself a *prophet of God*.

The movement spread extensively in the East, and it had a large following in some sections of the West, notably in North Africa. It appears to have gathered in a good many Marcionite Christians in certain places, and they, in turn, probably gave fresh ideas to the movement. It must have had real vitality and a fairly solid body of ideas to have held the interest of such a brilliant youth as Augustine for nine years at the formative stage of his life. There can be no question that his mind was more deeply infected and tinged by its major doctrines than he himself ever suspected. His feeling about marriage and the propagation of human life is very close to that of this dualistic sect ; his belief that an unbaptised infant is a mass of sin points in the same

ANTI-CHURCH HERESIES AND SCHISMS

direction, while the scope and sphere which he assigns to Satan looks strangely like an unconscious adoption of a page out of the creed of Manichæan dualism. It is an interesting historical fact that, while the Manichæan movement from its very origin was sympathetic with all the Gnostic heresies and anti-Church sects, it was everywhere intensely hostile to the Roman Catholic Church and thought of it as the offspring of Satan and as inspired by his kingdom of darkness.[1] We shall find, too, that all the dualistic movements which emerged from the East in later times and spread through the West, propagated in altered and transformed fashion the fundamental nucleus of ideas here reviewed, and, plainly influenced by Manichæism, were strenuous anti-Church movements.

The Paulicians, unlike the Manichæans, were Christians, though they were very positively opposed to the Roman Catholic Church. They show some affiliation in ideas with the Manichæans and with the followers of Marcion, though they probably had an independent origin, and they are less dualistic. Some authorities suppose that they were called Paulicians because, like the Marcionite Church, they exalted the position of St. Paul and his anti-legalistic attitude. It is, however, much more likely that they are named from Paul of Samosata, with whose views about the nature of Christ they were in sympathetic accord. They appear to have emerged from the

[1] See Harnack's *Hist. Dog.*, Vol. III., p. 331.

THE CHURCH'S DEBT TO HERETICS

confusion of sects in the Byzantine Empire, early in the fifth century, though we have little information about them before the seventh century. They formed a blend of ideas drawn from the Marcionites, the Manichæans, the Adoptionist heretics, and withal they developed a temper hostile to the Church. Instead of being innovators, as used to be supposed, they were, on the contrary, over-conservative and old-fashioned. They were entrenched in a world-outlook that belonged to the early period of Christian thought, as it was in their isolated regions, and when at a later time they came in contact with the developed Church they set themselves against its innovations. They were opposed to the worship of the Virgin Mary, and also to the worship of saints and images. They insisted upon adult baptism, as against the baptism of infants. They put the authority of Scripture above the authority of the Church. They rejected the Roman Catholic priesthood and hierarchy, and attacked the monastic life. They refused to distinguish in garb between the clergy and the laity, and they used simple, natural titles for their spiritual leaders. They reveal the inevitable antagonism felt by an older and simpler form of faith toward a developed dogmatic and ritualistic system.

Their early stage of history is obscure. They probably lived apart from the great currents of life and movement, hidden away beyond the Taurus mountains in south-eastern Armenia, where their heresy attracted little attention. But early in the ninth

ANTI-CHURCH HERESIES AND SCHISMS

century large numbers of these Paulicians, probably not less than 100,000, were transported from their retreats in Armenia into Thrace, to form a buffer along the Danube, and by thus using them as a defence against visible foes the Christian world gave them an opportunity to spread invisible forces over Europe. F. C. Conybeare, in his translation of a manual of the Paulician Church in Armenia, called *The Key of Truth*, which was written about 800, has supplied us with much new material about this mysterious sect, and in his extensive Introduction he has made an important contribution to our knowledge of the views and practices of these heretics. He has brought out very emphatically the adoptionist character of the Paulician faith. They held that Jesus was born as a man, though He was, they believed, a new creation. At His baptism, when He had fulfilled all righteousness, He was anointed the Messiah by the Holy Ghost, and was chosen to be God's only and well-beloved Son. He was thus not God, but a newly-created Adam and the beginner of a new spiritual race.

They considered Christ's baptism to be the true form of baptism for all His followers, and they, therefore, denied the legitimacy of the baptism of infants. Their Church, which they called "the holy universal and apostolic Church," consisted for them of persons who had received baptism in faith and who preserved unbroken the apostolic traditions. They believed that the Holy Spirit entered the

THE CHURCH'S DEBT TO HERETICS

Christian at the moment of his baptism, and that by this act he *became* a Christian, *i.e.*, in his measure a Christ. They regarded the word " Trinity " as unscriptural. They denied the reality of Purgatory ; they did not believe in the intercession of saints for the dead ; they condemned as idolatrous the use of images, pictures, crosses, incense or candles. They maintained that the Roman Catholic Church had " corrupted " the rite of baptism, and had lost the efficacy of its own orders and its sacraments, and thus was no longer the Church. They themselves had a single grade of ecclesiastics, whom they called the *Elect*. Unlike the Manichæans, who used the same term, the Paulicians required that their elect persons should be married and should be fathers of families. The elect were recipients of the Spirit as Christ had been at the Jordan.

These views, or similar ones, were in evidence almost everywhere in Europe in the twelfth and thirteenth centuries, and we shall see that many forms and types of anti-Church movements came into operation, often with sudden and surprising potency, during the Middle Ages. The Paulicians appear in Church documents under a variety of names. They are often called Publicani, and by this latter name they were condemned in 1179 in the third Lateran Council. They were condemned as Paulicians at the Council of Oxford in 1160, and the Chronicle of Gulielmus, which reports their condemnation, says : " They took their rise in Gascony from some

ANTI-CHURCH HERESIES AND SCHISMS

unknown author and have multiplied like the sand of the sea in France, Spain, Italy and Germany !"[1]

Another branch of this great Ygdrasil tree of heresy was the sect of the Bogomils. They were, in reality, only a Bulgarian variety of the general far-flung dualistic, anti-Church movement, and they constituted a kind of bridge between the Far Eastern and the distinctly Western heretical sects. They were the result of a missionary enterprise on the part of the Paulicians in the Taurus, who effectively invaded Bulgaria with their message in the ninth century. The Bogomils are more obviously dualistic than the Paulicians appear to be in *The Key of Truth*, but the former sect shows quite conclusively that the entire movement, in all its varied branches and ramifications, goes back to the dualistic roots of the Gnostics and the Manichæans. The name Bogomil is of uncertain origin. It may mean " Beloved of God," and thus be much like the European term, " Friends of God," but it is more probable that the sect was named from a prominent Bulgar leader named Bogomil. The same movement in the Far East was called in Syriac, Massaliani. It would appear that out of these Balkan states have emerged not only wars that have desolated Europe, but heresies also that have undermined whole regions of the Roman Catholic faith.

Once more we find strong adoptionist tendencies, opposition to the worship of Mary and the venera-

[1] Quoted from Conybeare, *op. cit.*, p. cxxxix.

THE CHURCH'S DEBT TO HERETICS

tion of saints, with a disapproval of the use of images, relics and the crucifix. The Bogomils regarded the baptism of the Roman Catholic Church as like that of John at Jordan—a baptism with water and not with the Spirit. Those who took it, as those who took John's baptism, were "Pharisees." The mass, too, was considered a sacrifice to demons and not a spiritual service. Their own *Elect* were, they believed, the true spiritual successors of the Apostles. They continued the ancient Manichæan and Gnostic mythology about creation. They held that Satanael, a fallen heavenly being whom they identified with the God of Moses and the Pentateuch, created the earth. He also made man, but he was unable to do more than create the body. At this crisis God—the real God—intervened and breathed a soul into the body which Satanael had made. God did this on the condition that the new race should belong to Him and fill the places vacated in heaven by the fallen angels. Satanael, to defeat God's plan, seduced Eve and brought forth by her an offspring of his own, Cain, while Abel was the normal child of Adam and Eve. In the course of time the good God, who until then had been the *unknown God*, sent forth His Logos, who entered the world through the Virgin Mary, but with an ethereal body, not a truly human body. Satanael plotted His death, but without knowing that Christ had a body which could neither suffer pain, nor be killed. Christ triumphantly survived the ordeal and was raised gloriously to heaven,

ANTI-CHURCH HERESIES AND SCHISMS

while Satanael, beaten and defeated, lost the *el* from his name, lost his power, and became henceforth just poor, plain Satan !

Next come the Cathari, sometimes called Patarenes, Bulgars, Tixerands and Albigenses. The list of dualistic heretics in the Middle Ages reads almost like a passage from the Book of Joshua : " The living God is among you and He will drive out from before you the Canaanite, the Hittite, the Hivite, the Perizzite, the Girgashite, the Amorite and the Jebusite." The Cathari (a word which means the *Pure*, or *Puritans*) were formed out of the thousand-year wreckage and *débris* of many earlier movements scattered over both East and West. They show everywhere a marked dualistic strain, some of them holding that the forces of good and evil are equally balanced ; others, probably the majority of them, holding that the good in the end will overcome the powerful element of evil. They believed that an evil God, Satan, was the instigator of many of the events and doings recorded in the Old Testament, and that this same evil-minded being is the creator of *this* world, which is actually now either purgatory or hell ; purgatory for some, hell for others. In the next world, which is God's world—the world of Spirit—there will be peace and joy and salvation. The Cathari endured this world, therefore, as a hard and necessary stage of life on their way to their true heavenly home, where at last they would be freed from the body with its burden of ill and evils. Christ is the new Adam, the instrument of the Spirit, and men who are to be saved must become *new creatures*, like Him, partakers of the Spirit. John the Baptist, with his material baptism, they held, represented the old order, a continuation of the Old Testament system. Christ introduced a wholly new order, a spiritual order, revealing the God of love and truth and light. They pointed out that those who had received only water baptism in the apostolic period (see Acts viii. 15-16) were imperfect and external until they received the Spirit. They sometimes carried their opposition to external things to the point of holding that God dwells not in houses made with hands. A Church is not a house of stones and mortar ; it is a company of persons who live by the Spirit. Their membership was divided into two groups, a larger group, called " the believers," and a smaller one composed of " the perfect." " The perfect," who were both men and women, had received the gift of the Spirit, they were " the elect," " the initiated," " the consoled." They had the Abba-crying spirit, they formed the true priesthood and they could administer the *consolamentum*, the baptism with Spirit and Fire, which absolves from all sin and restores to the soul of the recipient the lost garment of immortality, the covering which is from heaven. These *perfecti* took vows of absolute chastity. They held that family must be sacrificed for the kingdom of Christ. They regarded the begetting of offspring as a positive evil,

ANTI-CHURCH HERESIES AND SCHISMS

and they abstained from all food which they believed to be sexually begotten—meat, milk, eggs, butter and cheese.[1] Their extreme ascetic tendency indicates a long line of past inheritances, and many of their customs reveal primitive traits which carry them back in origin to the earliest period of Christian history, if not to movements that antedate the birth of the Church. St. Bernard of Clairvaux, who had a holy horror of their heresy, bears this fine testimony to their lives : " If you interrogate them, nothing can be more Christian ; as to their conversation, nothing can be less reprehensible, and what they speak they prove by deeds. As for the morals of the heretic, he cheats no one, he oppresses no one, he strikes no one ; his cheeks are pale with fasting, he eats not the bread of idleness, his hands labour for his livelihood."

They were eager proselytisers, fervid missionaries, and they carried their views into every part of Europe. They had no fear of death. They had faced the worst, and they believed that the best awaited the soul that dared to die for the faith. This world was, in any case, an enemy's country, and the real fatherland was yonder, where the martyr fire would send them. Under no circumstances would they tell a lie, of course not to save their own lives. They would not kill. They would not commit an impure act. They shrank from no efforts or labours. They lived by simple occupations and practised a

[1] Strangely enough they made an exception of fish.

THE CHURCH'S DEBT TO HERETICS

quiet, unobtrusive way of life. Many of them were weavers, hence the frequent name for the sect of " Tixerands " or " Tisserands," *i.e.*, weavers. They were excessively anti-Church in their views and attitudes, and they furnished a powerful, silent support and background to those within the Church who were eager to reform it or transform it. They were opposed primarily to the moral standards and practices of the Church. They disapproved of masses, of pilgrimages, of indulgences. They did not recognise the validity of ordination or of the hierarchy or of the sacraments. They claimed that the entire Church system was a continuation of the inadequate dispensation of John the Baptist, and therefore without Spirit, Life or Power.

It would have been a negligible matter if there had been only here and there a scattered heretic with views like these and an unconquerable spirit of opposition such as they showed. But they were not few, they were many. They had come originally across the Balkans, through Dalmatia, into Italy. They were solidly entrenched in their views and habits of mind, they had very strict ideals of life, they were efficient, diligent workers, they had more than average mental ability and they steadily made their way. They spread northward from Italy and gradually penetrated France, the Rhine Valley, the Low Countries, and, to a small extent, Great Britain, but their great *habitat* was in Southern France. This section of Europe was in many ways a unique civili-

ANTI-CHURCH HERESIES AND SCHISMS

sation. It was the rival of Paris and Northern France. It was the land of Troubadours and Courts of Love, a nursery of imagination and adventure. It had its own poets, philosophers and doctors. Its people loved freedom and individual rights, and they did not take kindly to the dominance of the Church. It was here that the spirit of the Cathari found its best support and its widest sweep. Here they received the name Albigenses or Albigeois. The name derives from the cathedral city of Albi, not far from Toulouse, in the Province of Narbonne. This had been Arian territory in the days of the Goths. It had also been overrun by the Mohammedan invaders in the eighth century. The inhabitants had taken naturally and kindly to Paulician and Bogomil doctrines, and from the eleventh century onward it was a region decidedly favourable to the views of the Cathars—and here the desperate battle between Church and heretics was eventually to be fought out in its fiercest fashion. I shall deal in the next chapter with the long struggle between the Church and its varied foes. This chapter merely presents, in the briefest compass, the background and environment which help to explain the diverse types of heresy which from the year 1200 grew like mushrooms in all Christian lands and could not be exterminated by fire, or force, or inquisition.

CHAPTER VIII

A HARVEST OF SECTS AND SCHISMS

WHEN Hildebrand—Pope Gregory VII.—died in 1085 it seemed to all pious observers as though the supremacy of the Church was settled for all time and as though its unity had now at length been permanently achieved. On the contrary, the new century then about to open, the twelfth, was to see the beginning of a battle with heresy and schism which was to know no truce and no terminus. It is still going on unabated.

There were many historical causes operating to produce this situation, though they were not explicitly seen and recognised in the closing years of Hildebrand's century. The most sensitive spiritual observers knew that all was not well in Zion, and there were already announcements of prophetic warning, but they were little heeded. The lax morals of the celibate clergy, the crude and unspiritual state of the people in general, the absence of preaching and constructive effort, substitution of external systems and practices for inward and living experience, all tended to work toward spiritual disaster. Besides the sapping internal weaknesses, always operating within the body, there were inva-

A HARVEST OF SECTS AND SCHISMS

sions of heretical thought which were beginning to come insidiously from outside the fold itself. We have seen in the preceding chapter what an environment of heretical ideas was slowly forming almost everywhere around the Christian groups, and now we shall see what quite naturally emerged from that environment. Then there came, as unpredictable as the direction of the wind in spring, movements of thought, the blowing of the Spirit, the birth of novel ideals, the leadership of dynamic personalities, which carried individuals and groups often farther than they had expected to go, and toward conclusions of which they themselves had no suspicion when they took their first forward steps. I shall begin this chapter with a brief review of the life and work of one of these " dynamic personalities " who did much to produce a critical rationalistic temper of mind, to unsettle dogmatic quiet, to encourage free thought, and to foment the leaven of new ideas, and to *make* heretics whether he was one or not—I mean Peter Abelard, " Master Peter," as his disciples called him.

He was born at Le Pallet, in Brittany, eleven miles from Nantes, in 1079. His family, a noble one, intended him for a military career, but he took matters into his own hand, and from his early youth dedicated himself to learning, saying, " I prefer the strife of disputation to the trophies of war." He studied for a short time under the famous nominalist Roscellin, whose doctrine was eventually condemned

THE CHURCH'S DEBT TO HERETICS

because it seemed inconsistent with the doctrine of the Trinity. Abelard turned from Roscellin, the most extreme nominalist, to the most extreme realist of the time, and attached himself to the Cathedral School in Paris, presided over by the renowned, though crude, teacher, William of Champeaux. Abelard possessed a native bent for questioning, for criticism, for doubt. He was the greatest dialectician of his time, a genius in debate, gifted with amazing precocity and subtlety. He saw at once the weak points in the logic of William of Champeaux, and he perceived how easy it would be to make the famous teacher's doctrine absurd and ridiculous. He proceeded to win his easy triumph. Having succeeded in dissipating the glory of this master, Abelard carried away his disciples and became himself the far-famed teacher of the time, first at Melun, then at Corbeil, and later at St. Geneviève, an abbey of secular canons outside the city limits. He had a " fatal impulse to annoy," and he interrupted his own teaching at various times in order to harass and humiliate distinguished rival teachers, over whom, according to his own accounts, he won signal dialectical victories. His own most brilliant period was that between 1108 and 1118, when young men from all over Europe flocked to Paris to study with this bold and interesting teacher who had carried off the victory over all other teachers of the age.

It was when he was at the height of his intellectual

A HARVEST OF SECTS AND SCHISMS

fame that he had a " fall " which tinged and coloured all the rest of his career, and which, in its far-reaching effects, brought defeat to his ambitious plans and played havoc with the issues of his life. The immortal story of the love of Heloise does not need to be retold. In the pathetic autobiography of Abelard—*History of my Misfortunes*—and in the letters between Abelard and the wonderful woman whose name is forever linked with his, the romance and the tragedy are painted in undying colours. Abelard's " confessions " leave us with a feeling of pity, but also with a feeling of horror and a sense of his moral weakness and selfishness which nothing can relieve. He was morally undisciplined, vain, proud and self-centred. He towered intellectually above all the men of his century, and he trained a whole generation of thinkers, but he lacked the moral fibre and the spiritual wisdom which make a truly great soul.

Heloise took the veil at Argenteuil and Abelard withdrew to the Abbey of St. Denys, where, as was to be his destiny henceforth, he found little peace, and he soon left the quarrels and contentions of the abbey for a quiet retreat. His students remained loyal to him throughout all his dark days, and they urged him to return to his vocation as teacher. He answered their call with a treatise from his pen, not confining himself to problems of philosophy but boldly dealing with central questions of theology. It was a work *On the Divine Unity and Trinity*, a

THE CHURCH'S DEBT TO HERETICS

subject bristling with dangers. His many rivals and enemies now turned upon him and charged him with grave errors and heresies. He was tried *in absentia* at the Synod of Soissons in 1121 and was condemned. His book was ordered to be burnt, and he was imprisoned. He had insisted upon the unity of the Divine Nature, and he had treated the revelation of God under three modes or aspects, Power, Wisdom and Love, much after the manner of Sabellius. He was largely influenced in his views by the Neo-Platonic doctrine of the one supreme Good; the Nous, or Reason, of God, and the World-Soul. One of the main charges made against him at the Synod was that he had presumed to lecture on the mystery of the Trinity without being authorised by the Church to do so.

He was soon allowed to return to St. Denys but he quickly produced a new storm, a cyclone in fact, by undertaking to prove, quite rightly as we now know, that St. Denys, *i.e.*, St. Dionysius, their founder, was not, as everybody supposed, the first bishop of Athens. The pride of the monks could not stand such a shock, and Abelard was forced to flee from the abbey to avoid the consequences of the anger of the holy brothers. He built himself a lonely wattled cell not far from the city of Troyes, but multitudes of students, both old and new ones, found out his retreat and gathered around the beloved master. He rebuilt and enlarged his cell, which became a busy centre, with huts and tents about it,

A HARVEST OF SECTS AND SCHISMS

forming a *School*, which was dedicated to the Paraclete. He later turned his Oratory of the Paraclete over to Heloise and her band of nuns as their spiritual home, while he withdrew to become Abbot of St. Gildas on a desolate part of the coast of Brittany. This proved to be no shelter of peace, but rather another rough and stormy stage in a troubled life.

Nothing seemed able, however, to check the creative power of his fertile mind. His literary activity continued. In the period of semi-quiet which followed upon his withdrawal from St. Gildas he wrote his *Dialectic*, a book of immense importance in the history of human thought. He wrote also at this time that extraordinary book, *History of my Misfortunes*, a new type of " Confessions," and another trouble-provoking book, *An Introduction to Theology*. The boldest of all his disturbing contributions was his book entitled, *Sic et Non*—" Yes and No." It consisted of parallel passages selected from the Bible and the authoritative Church Fathers, showing that as much can be said on one side of any great issue as on the other, since the authorities are mutually conflicting and so neutralise one another.

It was also in this period of semi-peace that Abelard returned to his work of teaching, which always had a fascination for him. It was at this time, probably at St. Geneviève, that some of the most famous men of that generation came to study with him, the most notable among them being the great English scholar, John of Salisbury. In the group of disciples was Peter Lombard, whose *Sentences* became one of the main intellectual forces for the next three hundred years. William of Conches and Gilbert de la Porée were two more scholars who caught and shared his spirit of honest inquiry. His influence never ceased to work until the aim of his life was achieved, and indeed transcended, in the age of the Renaissance. Arnold of Brescia was a devoted disciple, but his connection dated from an earlier period of the master's life. Abelard's method of thought, his boldness, his rationalism, his antagonism to dogma, his resolve to count nothing settled had a decided effect upon the bold spirits of his age and made his school a nursery of heresy. His doctrines were full of challenges to the pious, the orthodox, the saintly. He displayed the modern temper of mind. He carried reason far beyond the bounds where most scholastic thinkers stopped. He reversed Anselm's motto, *credo ut intelligam*, and insisted that knowledge should fortify and guide faith —*intelligo ut credam*. He disregarded authorities and names, as vain things for safety. He opened up and freshly re-interpreted the most ancient and sacred doctrines.

Abelard had long felt that he should some day come into collision with Bernard of Clairvaux, the supreme figure of the century and one of the greatest saints of all Christian history. They were "incommensurable" men, formed on wholly different models, different "patterns in the mount." St.

A HARVEST OF SECTS AND SCHISMS

Bernard was spurred on to the attack by enemies of Abelard, but on his own account he was profoundly disturbed by the spirit of criticism, rationalism, doubt and questioning which prevailed in Abelard's circle. The very success of Abelard's teaching distressed the saint. "His books cross the seas. They go over and beyond the Alps. They fly from province to province, from kingdom to kingdom. Everywhere they are received with enthusiasm. It is even supposed that they are honoured and prized at the court of Rome."[1] He saw in the bold critic a defiance of all authority, and he felt that every holy teaching of the Church was in danger from this man, who knew no limits to the sphere of reason. Abelard himself had said: "When it is a question which concerns truth or science I never obey customs, I obey reason."[2] St. Bernard hesitated to enter the fight, but when once he made up his mind for the attack upon the giant he intended it to be a fight to the death. He carried forward his war of faith against reason with all the force and fury of a crusade. He had a shining mark and he was minded to win. Abelard saw at once when he entered the Council of Sens that he had no chance of victory. The decision was predetermined. He withdrew from Sens not only condemned, but an old and broken man, though hardly more than sixty.

Peter the Venerable, a serene and gentle saint, a

[1] St. Bernard's *Letters*, No. CCCXXVI.
[2] Quoted from Hauréau, *Hist. Phil. Scol.*, Part I., p. 384.

man with a human heart rather than a scent for heresy, received the defeated scholar at the Abbey of Cluny, and cared for him like a real brother. Humbly the broken man wrote to Heloise : " I do not want to be an Aristotle if that would separate me from Christ, for there is no other name than His under heaven through which I can be saved. I adore Christ. With the arms of faith I embrace Him." After a year at Cluny his health failed so seriously that he was moved for a better climate to Chalon where, in the spring of 1142, he passed into a peace which he had never known on earth. Peter the Venerable bore this fine testimony of him : " He is ever to be named with honour, the servant of Christ, verily Christ's philosopher."[1] Abelard was a genius in the truest sense, and his overtopping intellectual greatness would have brought him into collision with orthodox authority even if he had not merited trouble from his moral weaknesses and his personal vagaries. He was, however, never a disloyal son of the Church. He loved Christ with a devoted passion, but he was a born innovator ; he could not follow track ; he introduced new ideas, new interpretations, a new type of authority, a new freedom, and he insisted on " liberty of judgment."

One of the outstanding " errors " for which he was condemned, both by the Council and later by the Pope, was his " new view " of the Atonement, a view which multitudes of modern Christians hold.

[1] Poole, *Illustration of the Hist. of Med. Thought* (2nd ed.), p. 145.

A HARVEST OF SECTS AND SCHISMS

The following proposition was pronounced to be heretical, both negatively and positively, by both authorities : " I think that the purpose and cause of the incarnation was that Christ might illumine the world by His wisdom and arouse it to a love of Himself."[1] Another passage taken from the extracts of his condemnation says : " To us it appears that we are none the less justified in the blood of Christ and reconciled to God by this singular Grace exhibited to us in that His Son took our nature, and in it took upon Himself to instruct us alike by word and example even unto death, *and so bound us to Him by love*; so that kindled by so great a benefit of Divine grace, love should not be afraid to endure anything for His sake."[2]

In a striking passage in his *Commentary on Romans* Abelard says : " Every man is made juster, that is to say, becomes more loving to the Lord after the passion of Christ [*i.e.*, after his knowledge of it], than he was before, because a benefit actually received kindles the soul into love more than one merely hoped for. Our redemption, therefore, is that supreme love of Christ shown to us by His passion, which not only frees us from slavery and sin, but acquires for us the liberty of sons of God, so that we fulfil all things, not so much from fear as from love of Him who exhibited such great love toward us."[3]

---

[1] *Petri Abaelardi Opera*, Ed. by Cousin (Paris, 1849–59), Vol. II., p. 767.
[2] *Ibid.*, II., p. 767.
[3] Taken from Rémusat's *Abélard, Sa Vie*, etc., Vol. II., pp. 412–414. The *Comm. on Romans* is in Cousin, *Opera*.

THE CHURCH'S DEBT TO HERETICS

The extracts given above are more or less cold and abstract, but Abelard's famous *Fifth Letter to Heloise* is touched with deep emotion and throbs with a vital personal experience, which shows plainly enough that for him the atonement was much more than a theory. He writes : " Art thou not moved to tears or to compunction by the only begotten of God, who, having done no wrong, was for thy sake and for all, seized by most impious men and dragged away and scourged and with covered face mocked, smitten with the hand, spat upon, crowned with thorns, and at length hung between thieves on the gibbet of the Cross, then so disgraceful, and slain by the sort of death which was then most appalling and accursed ? Have Him, my sister,—thine own and the Church's true spouse—have Him before thine eyes, carry Him in thy mind ! Gaze upon Him as He goes out to be crucified for thee, laden with His own Cross. . . . Suffer thou with Him who suffered willingly for thy redemption, and be thou pierced with Him who was crucified for thee. . . . He is Himself the way by which the faithful pass out of exile to their home. . . . He has bought thee, not with what is His, but with Himself. With His own blood He bought thee and redeemed thee. . . . What, I ask, did He see in thee—He who has lack of nothing—that to win thee He did battle, even to the agonies of a death so full of horror and of shame ? What, I say, does He seek in thee except thyself ? He is the 'true Lover, who longs for thyself, not for anything that is thine. He is the true Friend, who said Himself, when ready to die for thee, 'Greater love hath no man than this, that a man lay down his life for his friends.' "[1]

Abelard had not only discarded the ancient theory that Christ made atonement to the Devil, but he had attained the insight that *no* expiation was needed and no substitutionary sacrifice was required. The coming of Christ and His dying in our behalf is the miracle of Grace, and the effect of it is the redemption and moral transformation of those who see and feel the significance of this amazing gift of love. The whole work of Christ is thus vital and spiritual, not to execute a *scheme*. Here in germ, if not something more, is the profoundest modern view of the atonement, and here at last we feel as firm a grasp of the humanity of Christ as of His divinity. Bernard may have been of stronger moral fibre than his opponent was, and he may have more truly deserved the title of " saint," but he knew less clearly what the atonement meant than did the man whom he branded as " heretic." The fact that Abelard had sinned, had suffered, had repented, had been forgiven, and had been saved by grace, made the old traditional doctrine impossible and inadequate for him, and in a flash of insight he reached through to reality and found a deeper and a truer interpretation.

---

[1] I have quoted the letter much abbreviated, and have used Canon R. C. Moberley's translation as given in his *Atonement and Personality*. pp. 377-378.

THE CHURCH'S DEBT TO HERETICS

When Abelard was summoned to Sens for his final trial, Arnold of Brescia, one of his most devoted disciples and friends, joined him of his own accord, and at the risk of his own life stood faithfully by him. St. Bernard of Clairvaux, writing to Pope Innocent in 1140, says : " Goliath [Abelard] advances, tall of stature, clad in the armour of war, preceded by his armour-bearer, Arnold of Brescia."[1] In another letter of the same year, written to the Bishop of Constance, Bernard says : " I speak of Arnold of Brescia, and I wish he were of as sound doctrine as he is of strict life. And if you wish to know more, he is a man who comes neither eating nor drinking, but with the devil alone he is hungering and thirsting for the souls of men. . . . Up to the present time, in whatever place he has lived, he has left such foul and destructive tracks that he dares not return to any place wherever he has imprinted his footmark."[2]

Arnold was born in Brescia about the year 1100. Otto of Freising, in his *Gesta*, says that Arnold studied with Abelard, and Bernard again and again links their names.[3] He was possessed of " quick intelligence," the spirit of an innovator. He was, as Bernard says, a true fellow-mate to Abelard. He went back to the Gospel story of the love of God in Christ as the heart of Christianity. That faith in

[1] Letter CLXXXIX.
[2] Letter CXCV.
[3] *Gesta Friderici imperatoris* in *Mon. Ger. Hist.*, XX., p. 403.

A HARVEST OF SECTS AND SCHISMS

Divine love was the spring of his life. He joined with it, too, an intense love for his human fellows—the plain, everyday, common man—a love which was to reach its full height a little later in Francis of Assisi. He was pure-minded, and amid all pitfalls and moral dangers he must have kept pure to have won such words as the above from the great heresy-hater, St. Bernard.

He aspired to lead a Christ-like life, and to accomplish that purpose he entered a monastery in Brescia, was ordained a priest, and rose to be prior of the community of canons regular to which he belonged. He lived a life above reproach, and was distinguished both by character and intellect. He was a solid and serious student of the Gospels and of the primitive Church. He seems to have formed his idea of a pure and holy Church, freed from worldliness and corruption, from his study of the New Testament. He had the vision and the spirit of a real reformer. Unlike most monks of the time, he entered heart and soul into the problems of the city. He was very sensitive to the sufferings and tragedies of the common people, who usually counted for very little. The Lombard cities were awakening to the possibilities of large municipal freedom, and Brescia shared that hope and aspiration. Arnold, with his fervour and eloquence, soon became the incarnation of this movement, and he rose to be the recognised leader of the new-born democratic spirit. The supreme obstacle, however, to any real freedom of action and power was the bishop, the prince of the region, the great landed proprietor, entrenched in his hereditary rights and authority.

Thinking on his problem night and day, and brooding over the wrongs and sufferings of the common people, whose redemption and welfare rested lightly on the Church, this fiery and glowing champion leaped to the revolutionary conclusion that bishops and other clerics should be spiritual guides, and not temporal rulers and controllers of human destiny. The only way back, he believed, to true apostolic and evangelic piety and real religion was through the path of primitive poverty and surrender on the part of the hierarchy. Only by a return to poverty could the clergy become spiritual followers of Christ and servants of the people ; only by a complete change of their economic status could the larger freedom of life be won.

During the absence of the Bishop of Brescia from his diocese on a visit to Rome, there was an insurrection, led apparently by Arnold, and an attempt was made to prevent the bishop from returning again to his temporal power.[1] Arnold was exiled by decree of the Lateran Council in 1139, but, as we have seen, he rushed to Abelard's side at Sens, where he shared the condemnation of his master, though he seems to have escaped imprisonment. After a

[1] The sources of information are Otto's *Gesta* and the *Historia Pontificalis* by John of Salisbury, printed in *Mon. Ger. Hist.*, Vol. XX.

A HARVEST OF SECTS AND SCHISMS

short period of retreat Arnold appeared in Paris as a lecturer on moral and religious questions, attracting a large group of hearers. John of Salisbury says of his teaching in Paris : " Arnold interpreted the Holy Scriptures. He showed those things that fit the law of Christ and he showed how different many things in the Church are from that law. He did not spare the bishops, but showed how they had gone astray through cupidity, soilure of life, and because they tried to build the Church of Christ with force, with fire and with blood." He did not spare the great name of St. Bernard, whom he charged, not with wealth and luxury certainly, but with the subtler sins of pride, vainglory and jealousy.

The great Abbot of Clairvaux pursued him again, and finally induced the King of France to expel Arnold from France. He fled to Zürich, and Bernard had him expelled from Switzerland. He fled to Bohemia, where he was kindly treated, though the wrath of the saint still followed him.[1] Arnold seems at this time to have made peace with the Church and to have submitted to authority. He returned to Italy, and almost at once inaugurated a new crusade against temporal power and wealth, this time carrying the fight against the Pope himself—Eugenius III. According to Otto of Freising, Arnold said that no part of the government of the city of Rome belonged to the Pontiff, who ought to have only

[1] Bernard's *Letter*, CXCVI., to the Papal Legate in Bohemia, describes Arnold's heresies.

THE CHURCH'S DEBT TO HERETICS

spiritual functions. Otto declares that : " The evils springing from this pernicious teaching grew to such a head that not only were the houses and splendid palaces of the Roman nobles and cardinals pulled down, but violent hands were laid by the furious populace on the sacred persons of the cardinals, and some were disgracefully injured." Evidently there was a very widespread and popular uprising at this time against the power of the clerical oligarchy. Eugenius was forced to leave Rome during the years 1146–1149, and the Roman democracy triumphed under the leadership of Arnold. He was excommunicated, but he went on enlarging the scope of his demands, namely, that the spiritual power should be subordinate everywhere to the temporal powers, and that the functions of clerics should be only spiritual. Frederick Barbarossa was won over by the Pope, and that doomed Arnold. He did not, however, at once come to his end. He lived through the short reign of Anastasius IV., but the new Pope, Adrian IV., took up his case vigorously. Arnold had been kept for a time a prisoner, but in some way secured his freedom, and was once more looked upon as " a prophet " of the time, as a person of divine inspiration and with a divine mission. The Pope got the Emperor Barbarossa to enter into an agreement that he would have Arnold seized by the secular power and handed over to the Roman curia for trial. There is little certain information about either his trial or his execution. There is an account

A HARVEST OF SECTS AND SCHISMS

of his death which says that he was hung and burnt, and the ashes thrown into the Tiber for fear lest the people might collect his ashes and honour them as the ashes of a martyr. An anonymous poem describes Arnold as holding the position that the Pope is no longer the real Apostolicus and, as he does not exemplify in his life the teachings of the Apostles, there is no obligation of reverence or obedience towards him. He further maintains the view (later held by Wyclif and the Waldenses) that unworthy priests lose the power of administering the sacraments.

Arnold of Brescia was as dedicated to the spiritual regeneration of the Church of Christianity as St. Bernard was. He was as pure in his spirit, and as lofty in his idealism, and certainly as humble-minded as the latter, but his way of approach was totally different and his fate was correspondingly different. Arnold was a great preacher of evangelical simplicity in the prevailing terms of his age—he was passionate for a pure Church. In his main contention he had Bernard, his greatest foe, on his side, for Bernard had written : " Who will grant me before I die to see the Church of God such as it was in the ancient days, when the Apostles cast their nets not to catch gold and silver, but souls." Dante, in his *De Monarchia*, in a loftier and more balanced way, proclaimed many of the ideals of Arnold. Nicoline, the modern Italian poet, has made Arnold the hero of one of his dramas. In Rome his bust has been put up in the garden of the Pincian Hill (1873), and in Brescia a statue in his honour and to his memory was erected in 1882.[1]

Arnold had a forerunner in the radical reformer, Peter of Bruys, who also was probably a disciple of Abelard.[2] His birth date is uncertain, but he was burned alive at St. Gilles, in the South of France, in 1126, and was without much doubt the founder of the heretical sect called Petrobrusians. He was an out-and-out Anabaptist, opposing the baptism of infants as unscriptural and also futile. Faith being essential for any religious act, nothing spiritual can be accomplished by putting water on a child too young to exercise faith. To prove his point he quoted Mark xvi. 16. Peter the Venerable wrote a book against him using such a weighty argument as this: " If baptism administered to children is without effect, then all the millions of children who have received it since the beginning of the Church are damned !"

Peter of Bruys attacked the claim that worship must be confined to churches and be controlled by the Church, quoting Christ's words to the Samaritan woman. He insisted as vigorously as George Fox did, that churches, *i.e.*, church buildings, are unnecessary, for the Church consists of the congregation of those who have faith in Christ, not of buildings of

---

[1] The most important modern treatment of Arnold of Brescia is an article by E. Vacandard in *Revue des questions historiques*, for 1884.
[2] See Carl Schmidt's *Histoire de Cathares*, I., p. 38.

HARVEST OF SECTS AND SCHISMS

stone and mortar. He set himself against the miracle of the Mass. He opposed the whole theory of acquired *merit* and set himself against all forms of superstition. He collected a number of crosses and burned them on the public square of St. Gilles. In 1126 he himself was seized and burned at the stake. Peter the Venerable reports that he said : " O people believe not the bishops, the priests and the clerks who, as in much else, seek to deceive you as to the office of the altar, where they lyingly pretend to make the body of Christ and give it to you for the salvation of your souls." His views were held and widely spread through the South of France by the Petrobrusians.[1]

Henry of Lausanne was a reforming monk who appeared in the *rôle* of a Hebrew prophet about 1101. He is first heard of at Le Mans, a little later at Poitiers and Bordeaux, still later he settled in Languedoc, where he had a great career and powerfully affected the people by his bold message. He flayed the corrupt clergy and pointed to their vices. He called men to a pure life and a way of sacrifice. He came into collision with St. Bernard, who writes about him with fury and venom. He declares that Henry is a scholar, was once a monk, but has become " apostate," " a ravening wild beast," " raging against the flock of Christ." He " shuts the way of Christ to the children of Christians and they are not allowed to enter the way of salvation," *i.e.*, he

[1] See Lea, *Hist. Inquis.*, Vol. I., p. 68.

THE CHURCH'S DEBT TO HERETICS

opposes infant baptism.[1] The Henricians, or followers of this Henry of Lausanne, were very numerous and widespread. They joined in most districts with the Petrobrusians in one common anticlerical heresy. They antedated St. Francis in their insistence on poverty as a way of holiness and they prepared the way for the Waldenses. St. Bernard painted a doleful picture of the havoc the heretics have wrought in the South of France, and with holy fervour he set forth on a spiritual mission to bring them back to the faith.[2] He aroused the authorities to pursue the arch-heretic Henry, who, as a result, was captured in 1148 and brought in chains before his bishop, though there is no evidence that he was burned at the stake—he probably died in prison.

Another, and far more influential, attempt to reform the Church by a return to the simplicity of Gospel Christianity, was the movement inaugurated by Peter Waldo about the year 1173. It contained very much the same body of ideas that have been reviewed in this and the preceding chapter, but it possessed a greater intensity of spiritual fervour and a deeper experience of the meaning of apostolic Christianity. Waldo himself was a rich merchant of Lyons, who passed through a profound religious crisis which changed his whole outlook on life and

---

[1] Bernard's *Letter*, No. CCXLI.
[2] See, for the dark picture, Bernard's *Letters*, Nos. CCXLI. and CCXLII.

A HARVEST OF SECTS AND SCHISMS

altered all his estimates of values. He took the path to spiritual religion which was, in his century, the most pervious one, and that was the way of "poverty." He renounced the world and consecrated his wealth to what he believed to be the highest cause of truth.

He was acutely sympathetic with the hard lot of the poor people "whom the Church taxed when they were orthodox and burned when they were heretics," and, furthermore, he had become disillusioned about the mission of the existing Church. It seemed to him a failure, a travesty of the New Testament ideal. It is practically certain that he had some direct contact with the unsettling forces and movements of the time, for when he broke with his past and turned to his constructive task he plainly enough revealed the influence upon him of the old dualistic and anti-Church heresies. What is new is his own personality, his spirit, his faith, his fervour, and his real love for the common people.

He set out preaching as a layman. He used his fortune to get parts of the New Testament translated into the popular Provençal tongue, to have many copies made for distribution and to prepare suitable propaganda for his bold venture. He quickly gathered followers and formed them into a band of lay-preachers. They called themselves "the Poor Men of Lyons," though they were given many popular nicknames, and in later history they have been usually called "Waldenses," from Waldo, or

THE CHURCH'S DEBT TO HERETICS

"Vaudois" from the Alpine valleys where they settled in large numbers at a later period. They were forbidden by the Archbishop of Lyons to preach, but they refused to obey his inhibition, and they went out into a cold and hostile world to meet all the hazards and dangers which awaited heretics in the twelfth century.

They multiplied and spread rapidly and were soon to be found in almost all Continental countries. They merged often with other similar sectaries and greatly swelled the general current of *dissent*. They perfected a simple organisation which was formed much after the model of the Cathari and earlier dualistic sects. The persons who were most gifted, and who gave their whole time and thought to religion, were called "the Perfect," or Majorales, or sometimes Barbes. They maintained a strict manner of life, though they did not, as some of their forerunners did, proscribe marriage. They refused, however, to take life for any cause or pretext. They would not swear, either in court or in conversation. They held firmly and conscientiously to exact truth and straightforward honest dealing, and they suffered immensely for these traits which soon came to be well-known marks for the identification of " heretics." The " perfect " often supported themselves with some menial occupation, such as cobbling, tinkering, or peddling, and some of them practised simple arts of medicine and surgery. These occupations enabled them to get into homes everywhere and

A HARVEST OF SECTS AND SCHISMS

secured them a natural *entrée* to the people whom they wished to reach.

The Waldenses were advocates of a Church composed entirely of spiritual members. They were, like the Donatists, opposed to secularisation, and they stood emphatically for purity of heart and life. They were, at first, exponents of the view that the transformation of the bread and wine into Christ's Body and Blood could be effected only by priests whose lives were clean and pure and whose faith was apostolic, but gradually they went to a more extreme position and opposed transubstantiation altogether. They denied the reality of purgatory, the value of relics and pilgrimages, the utility of indulgences and the propriety of the veneration of the Virgin or of saints. They were opposed to the long list of "expensive superstitions" of their time. They came very close to the later Protestant position, though they lacked the insight and leadership which could have equipped them for an adequate Reformation of the Church, even had the time been ripe for it. They possessed little knowledge of history, they had only a superficial knowledge of Scripture, almost no grasp of the profounder religious doctrines, and they were very weak in mystical experience. They were, furthermore, too much given to negations—"thou shalt nots." Where they were strong was in their positive moral insight and testimony. They were brave exponents of a better way of life. They loved and tried to follow the Sermon on the Mount.

THE CHURCH'S DEBT TO HERETICS

They were the forerunners of movements which burst forth in greater volume and power at the Reformation and afterwards, and they influenced in all periods some of the most important leaders of Christian thought, John Wyclif being the most striking instance.

The Waldenses were subjected to a continuous fire of pitiless persecution. Their purity of life, their conscientious scruples, their stern and overt opposition to many of the practices of the Church, made them easy marks for the heresy-hunters. But, as usual, their martyrs buttressed the new faith, enkindled the zeal, re-animated the spirit and cemented the fellowship as well as almost invariably won them new followers.[1] They spread in large numbers through the South of France, where in some localities they joined with other sects which were more or less kindred in principles and practices with themselves, while in other localities, where the heretical movements had not actually fused together, their influence was cumulative and swelled the total volume of hostility and opposition to the Church.

The Council of Verona, in 1184, reviewed the menacing condition of heresies which had accumulated in the southern provinces of France, and called upon the bishops of those regions to search their dioceses and to take steps if possible to weed out the tares. It was during the papacy of Innocent III.

[1] Dr. Lea has given in his *History of the Inquisition* extensive accounts of the sufferings of the Waldenses. See especially Vol. II.

A HARVEST OF SECTS AND SCHISMS

(1198–1216)—a momentous period—that the great crusade, known in history as the Albigensian Crusade for the extermination of heresy, was carried out. It is one of the most appalling chapters in the history of the Christian Church, and it leaves upon the historical student, as it does upon the general reader, a sense of shame and horror. There were mingled a large number of motives in the hearts of the leaders, and the springs of action which pushed on these armies of pitiless destruction, burning cities, spreading havoc, killing indiscriminately men, women and children, were too complicated to be psychologically analysed either by them then or by us to-day. Fury against heresy was one factor in the mission of terror and destruction, but it was only one of many factors. Simon de Montfort's name is for ever associated with the wholesale crime, but so, too, is the name of Innocent. They both believed that the Church could not rise to its place of power and splendour until those whom they called " the enemies of God " and " the emissaries of Satan " were annihilated, but at the same time they were both tangled up with political aims which helped to blind their eyes to the iniquities which, in the name of Christ, they were committing. When the bloody crusade finally came to an end many of the best moral lives in France had been wiped out, the civilisation of a great, fair region of the country had been wrecked, the method most incompatible with the spirit of Christ had been tried to the hilt—but heresy was as virile as ever, and the spirit which inquired for truth and which refused to take a stone for bread was still unconquered and unconquerable.

During the thirteenth and fourteenth centuries "the Spiritual Franciscans" developed into a pronounced anti-Church sect. When the word "Fraticelli" first came into use it had reference in the early stage to the Tuscan "Spirituals," who were the followers of Brother Ubertino of Casale, but it soon came to be applied as a general term for heretical Franciscans. They settled in considerable numbers in Provençe and Languedoc after the period of the Albigensian crusade, where Peter John Olivi, a writer of note and influence, became the heart and head of the movement in the south of France. He was born in 1248 in the diocese of Béziers, was educated in the University of Paris, joined the Franciscan Order, adhered to the strict party, and became the inspired and zealous leader of it. He was accused of heresy at the General Chapter of the Order, held at Strasbourg in 1282. The remainder of his life was full of stress and disturbance, and the controversy over the questions which he raised continued long after his death, which occurred at Narbonne in 1298. The most competent judge of his life and writings is the German Franciscan, Father Ehrle, who, on the whole, defends him and his teaching.[1] Linked in the same general struggle for the ideals of poverty and spiritual religion were

[1] *Petrus Johannis Olivi, sein Leben und seine Schriften.*

A HARVEST OF SECTS AND SCHISMS

the Franciscan "Spirituals," Michael of Cesena, Bonagrazia and William of Occam, the famous Nominalist. Rienzi, too, "the last of the Tribunes," was inspired to undertake his task by the vision and the ideals of the "Spirituals." The "Spirituals" were deeply influenced by the teaching of the Waldenses, and in some regions they adopted most of the tenets of the latter sect, and wherever they existed they became intensely hostile to the Church and irreconcilable with its position and its practices.

John XXII. became Pope at Avignon—a Pope of the "Babylonish Captivity "—in 1316, and almost at once plunged into a contentious controversy with the "Spirituals" which lasted to the end of his papal period in 1334. His reign was marked by the fierce civil war in Germany over the Imperial crown between the two claimants, Louis of Bavaria and Frederick of Austria. The "Spirituals" supported Louis of Bavaria, who was opposed by the Pope, and whose supporters were laid under an interdict, so that the problem became a political as well as a spiritual one, and many persons took sides with the "Spirituals" for political reasons. After defeating Frederick of Austria, the Pope's favourite, at the battle of Mühldorf in 1322, Louis marched into Italy as the leader of the Ghibelline forces. He issued a manifesto in which he named John "that heretic who calls himself Pope John XXII." "He has risen," the manifesto continues, "against the Lord

THE CHURCH'S DEBT TO HERETICS

Jesus Christ, His Mother and the Apostles, and has attempted to destroy the evangelical doctrine of perfect poverty, the beacon of our faith !" G. K. Chesterton, in his valuable little book on *St. Francis of Assisi*, says that when the Franciscan movement turned into a heresy "it was a narrow heresy." The mood of poverty, he says, "turned into a monomania." "The unpersuaded rump [the Fraticelli] remained without producing anything in the least calculated to remind anybody of the real St. Francis."[1] It is true that spiritual "rumps" grow "narrow," "monomaniac" and "fanatical," and this one showed that tendency, but there was often "a reminder of St. Francis" in the lives and words of the "Spirituals," and they added a real contribution to the ever-growing current that finally became the irresistible flood which produced the Reformation.

The greatest single forerunner of the Reformation, one of the major "prophets" of all Christian history, was John Wyclif (1320–1384). He was pronounced officially a "heretic" in 1415, his body was dug up and burned, but he died too soon for the martyr's crown. The longest and hardest struggle of his life was that against the evils which had accumulated from the monastic system, the loose, immoral traits of the wandering friars, and the lax, inadequate pastoral care of English churches. He was animated not only by a desire for a purer and

[1] *Op. cit.*, pp. 227–228.

A HARVEST OF SECTS AND SCHISMS

more spiritual religion, but also by an intense patriotism—an eager desire to lay the moral and spiritual foundations for a better, nobler England. He became, too, the life-long champion of national and individual rights against papal encroachments. In this controversy he developed his famous "dominion doctrine." In its simplest meaning it held that all dominion, rule, ownership and right to property are gifts from God, to whom all right of dominion belongs. The right to exercise rule, office, dominion, both civil and spiritual, continues only so long as the person who holds it continues in grace and renders the service which God expects of him. If he lives in sin, or fails to render service, he "forfeits dominion," *i.e.*, loses his right to hold his office—even though he be Pope. Thus, by his logic, Wyclif arrived at the position already held by the Waldenses, and he passed beyond it. He called vigorously for purity of life, loyalty of spirit and effective service in all who accept what should be apostolic ministry, from the lowest servant to the papal Head of the Church. Step by step his deepening faith, his maturing moral insight and the drive of his logic carried him farther on and brought him to a more perilous stage of championship. In 1380 he attacked the doctrine of transubstantiation in these unambiguous words: "I maintain that among all the heresies which have ever appeared in the Church, there was never one which was more cunningly smuggled in by hypocrites than this one,

THE CHURCH'S DEBT TO HERETICS

or which in more ways deceives the people ; for it plunders them, leads them astray into idolatry, and denies the teaching of Scripture." [1] From this point to the end of his life Wyclif was engaged in developing his anti-papal views, in organising the translation of the Bible, and in working out a method of popular itinerant ministry—the band of " evangelical men," who developed into the Lollards.

He was a broad and diligent scholar, a brave, fearless man, a pure and saintly soul, and he imparted not only a new theory of the Church, but, what was better still, a new moral earnestness, a new experience of Christ, a new appreciation of the Gospels, a new interpretation of Christianity, and he effectively laid his spirit upon a band of disciples who carried forward his work and propagated his faith, both in England and on the Continent, especially, of course, upon John Hus in Bohemia, until in the sixteenth century his reforming efforts found greater fulfilment.

One of the most extraordinary of all the heretics in the history of the Church was the warrior-maid of Domremy—now St. Joan of Arc. She was born about 1412, and died at the stake in 1431 as heretic and sorceress. Her heresy consisted of a claim to be guided by interior voices which, she insisted, were from God, mediated to her through her beloved saints. She was devoted to the Church in her simple way, loved its sacraments, its service and its ministry ;

[1] *Trialogus*, IV., ii.

A HARVEST OF SECTS AND SCHISMS

but she put her own divine guidance above everything else, and spoke and acted like an inspired prophet, whose " thus saith the Lord " outweighed, in her mind, all creeds, all external authority, even of Archbishops or Popes. She is a strange, fascinating and pathetic figure—both burnt and canonised by the Church ; both a warrior and a saint. She belongs in our list because she was unconsciously a forerunner of the prophets of individualism, a martyr for the inalienable right of the soul to hear directly the voice of God.

CHAPTER IX

HERETICAL MOVEMENTS IN THE REFORMATION PERIOD

THERE was, as we have seen, a steady cumulation of assaults upon the doctrine and the structure of the Church throughout the twelfth, thirteenth and fourteenth centuries. But through the ages the venerable imperial system stood essentially unaffected and unchanged. At the opening of the thirteenth century the physical and metaphysical writings of Aristotle first came into the hands of European scholars, who up to that time had possessed only his logic, and these new-found books were almost at once condemned as dangerous to Christian truth ; but through the constructive labours of Albertus Magnus—the one scholar to win the title " magnus " (1193–1280)—and his greater disciple, Thomas Aquinas (1224–1274), Aristotle became the official philosopher of the Church before the century was finished. Greek scholars, with their precious manuscripts, flocked to Western seats of learning, European scholars quickly caught the torch from them, and young men soon began to care for other things than dogma. They discovered that human thought was much wider than the problems which

THE REFORMATION PERIOD

busied the Church. They became interested in history for history's sake, in man for man's sake, in literature for its human appeal. The world awoke as at a vernal equinox, and came to a fresh renascence stage of life and thought. Men reflected, questioned, criticised, challenged and proceeded to pass beyond all the old frontiers. It was inevitable that the awakened interest in man and the advance of thought should sooner or later bring either a gradual transformation of the Church, or a violent and revolutionary break with it. Attempts were made in both of these directions—the former method was defeated ; the second method prevailed.

It is important to keep in mind the fact that throughout the fourteenth and fifteenth centuries there was widespread dissatisfaction with the Church. The so-called " Babylonish captivity " of the papacy at Avignon (1309–1377), followed by the " Great Schism " (1377–1418), were disasters from which the Church never wholly recovered. The antipapal sects were never suppressed. The moral and intellectual labours of John Wyclif and John Hus, and their disciples, produced a profound effect in all the northern countries of Europe. " The Friends of God," up and down the Rhine Valley, while perhaps not technically " heretics," as Wyclif and Hus were, were yet impressive popular advocates of *lay religion*, as against a hierarchy. They cultivated an intense faith in the immediate presence of the Holy Spirit. They maintained that there was an unlost and inalienable *Divine centre* in man's soul, and that an unordained man, or even a woman, responsive to the voice of God, can accomplish a thousand times more than an immoral and undevout priest or bishop can do. They went so far as to hold that God can find some way to save a pure and devout person, though he may be unbaptised and unconnected with the Church. " *God can baptise him in the holy desire of his will.*" [1] The greatest of all the " Friends of God," Meister Eckhart (c. 1260–1327), an extraordinarily popular preacher, did much to exhibit the power of spiritual religion, and also much to prepare the way for the Reformation. During the closing period of his life Eckhart was charged with holding twenty-eight heretical views, and he died without having his name cleared of unorthodoxy ; but he was, nevertheless, a profound lover of God and man, and he helped greatly to bring the day-dawn of a new era.[2] The " heresies," and also the " near heresies," had all tended to emphasise the importance of experience in religion, and they had also insisted upon a religion of life. They had returned to the Galilean ideals of life, and they had felt anew the practical significance of the Sermon on the Mount and the call to the Kingdom of God which is realised in man.

[1] This position was taken in the " Book of the Nine Rocks," and also in John Tauler's sermons. For details, see my *Studies in Mystical Religion*, Chapter XIII.
[2] I have a chapter on Eckhart in *Studies in Mystical Religion*, and also in *At One with the Invisible*, edited by E. H. Sneath (Macmillan, 1921).

THE REFORMATION PERIOD

This note of emphasis received its clearest expression in the powerful writings of the foremost humanist, Erasmus of Rotterdam (1466-1536). The dates of Erasmus' life mark that great era of reflection, doubt, criticism, challenge, and the passing of old frontiers. Columbus, Copernicus, Gutenberg, Magellan, Leonardo da Vinci, Raphael, Michelangelo, Albrecht Dürer, Sir Thomas More and Martin Luther, are some of his contemporaries who did memorable things. Erasmus felt more clearly than most of the men of his age how pitiably the Church was failing in its mission, though not more so than the great Italian humanist and martyr, Girolamo Savonarola. He saw the shame and hypocrisies, the moral diseases too, which marked those in high places. He saw it all and he dared to set it forth with vigour and with humour. Nobody since the days of the classical writers had wielded such a pen as he did. He soon had the world reading and applauding his books—and thinking as well as laughing.

His edition of the Greek New Testament, his Paraphrases, and his edition of the *Works of St. Jerome* opened up a new world almost as truly as Columbus did. It enabled men to see vividly the difference between primitive Christianity and the Christianity of the fifteenth century. Everywhere and always the great humanist scholar put the stress upon life and character, not on ecclesiasticism and doctrine. As strongly as Thomas à Kempis, though

THE CHURCH'S DEBT TO HERETICS

in a different way, he called for an imitation of Christ. He insisted on the practice of the Sermon on the Mount and on a personal and social realisation of the Kingdom of God. He has been called timid and Laodicean, compromising and indifferent. It has been charged that he was *afraid* to assist Luther and that he lacked the martyr spirit. It is true that he had but small stock of passion for martyr-fire. He wrote frankly to a friend in 1521 : " All men have not strength for martyrdom. I fear lest, if any tumult should arise, I should imitate Peter." But he was never indifferent, never unconcerned about the truth, never neutral where moral issues were at stake. He was engaged in an undertaking wholly different from that of Luther, an effort to reform the Church from within and to save it from the catastrophe of revolution and schism. He saw the storm coming ; he knew more clearly than most of his contemporaries what havoc a revolutionary reformation meant, and he quickly grasped the fact that Luther was making all the aims, aspirations and hopes of the humanist futile and unattainable. The last years of Erasmus' life from 1520 to 1536 are pitiable ones. He was caught in the fierce swirl between the two irreconcilable currents. Each extreme party saw him in false perspective and judged him to be in the opposite camp. He was blamed for whatever was done on either side. His merciless revelations about the condition of the Church made him seem to be a heretic to the conservative party, and his refusal to go forward with Luther made his name abhorred in the protestant wing. But through it all he was an honest fighter for the cause in which he had enlisted—the moral and spiritual transformation of the Church, its purification, its restoration to primitive ideals, and the rebuilding of the world on a more moral and rational foundation. Erasmus failed. Counsels of moderation were rejected. The explosive forces were liberated, and the Church which Erasmus tried to hold together was cleft in twain.[1]

Luther was a far more intense, impulsive and dynamic type of person than Erasmus. He was profoundly *religious*. Eternal issues were primary concerns with him. Sin and salvation were the two *foci* of his orbit, Heaven and hell, God and Satan, Grace and damnation, were as indubitable facts as life and death were. When he felt the push of a great religious motive he was carried onward by an almost irresistible propelling force which made no account of obstacles. " I should go to Worms if there were as many devils in the city as there are tiles on the roofs"; " I should go to Leipzig if it rained Duke Georges for nine days running," are sayings of his which illustrate his " motor-type " of disposition. He could not calmly rationalise, balance, compromise, delay action, plan for remote effects and be content with a slight gain here or a

[1] The best recent study of Erasmus is by Preserved Smith, *Erasmus: A Study of his Life, Ideals and Place in History* (1923).

little transformation there. One might as well have tried to persuade a volcano or an earthquake to be "reasonable"! He was concentrated human energy; explosive and seismic, an elemental force of nature. He was not designed to work in quiet patience for the aims and ideals of Humanism; he was forged with fiery heat to be a reformer, to be the beginner of a new epoch.

And yet Luther was deeply entrenched in the past. He was an inheritor and a transmitter far more than he was an originator of something new. He was the heir of the mediæval heretics. He was the executor of the legacies of Wyclif and Hus. He had drawn heavily, too, upon the precious contribution which the mystics of the two preceding centuries had made, and, furthermore, he was to the core an Augustinian, *i.e.*, an evangelical of the old order. One of the most important strands in his complex nature was the mystical strand. He loved Tauler's sermons and the beautiful little fourteenth-century book, known by the name of "Theologia Germanica." He ranked these next to the Bible, and they had much to do with the formation of his own fundamental religious life and experience. He did not belong himself in the order of contemplative saints and mystics. He was not inclined to trust inward lights and subjective leadings. He preferred external and objective authority, but he cared greatly for the demonstration of religion in life and action, and he found *that* in the mystics. They seemed to

THE REFORMATION PERIOD

him to have *real religion*. They had discounted what he came to call " works " ; they seemed to go straight to the one source of grace and power and to draw into themselves from beyond a converting and transforming energy which buoyed them up and enabled them to live an overcoming life. He found in them the positive, efficacious religion which he missed in normal, everyday Christians and which he wanted to restore to the Christianity of his time.

There is one important event in Luther's own life which is kindred to the mystic's experience, and it is, too, an event of first importance for understanding his career as a reformer. He came upon his central idea—the battle-idea of the Reformation—by a sudden insight, in a flash, as an illumination or personal revelation. The experience seems to have occurred, not at Rome in 1510, as we used to suppose, but in his study at Wittenberg, when he was preparing his lectures on the Epistle to the Romans in 1515. The *live idea* burst into his consciousness making him see that it is not by " works," nor by the accumulation of " merits," that a soul is saved from its sin ; it is by trust and confidence in the grace and love of God—a God whom Christ has once and for all revealed to be forgiving, tender, kind and loving. To see, to feel, to know, that God is like Christ, that we can count upon His forgiving love, and, having seen that, to accept it, take it, act upon it as ours, *that* is faith, in Luther's sense of the word. Faith is, thus, a fact of experience—something felt, known and tested within one's own soul, so that, as Luther said, in his *Commentary on Galatians*, " the soul possesses whatever Christ Himself possesses."

It was this first-hand discovery which made Luther the hero of his epoch and the fearless reformer that he became. It is this experience which lies behind the ninety-five battle-words of his Theses on Indulgences. It is this experience which beats and throbs through his early books: *Address to the Nobility of the German Nation* ; *The Babylonish Captivity of the Church*; and *The Liberty of a Christian Man*. It is this note that sounds clearly above all the voices and threats at the Diet, for as he himself said : " Faith makes a man intrepid, joyous and full of cheer." It was this insight that produced the great Luther whom we love—the Luther of 1515–1524. His grasp of the meaning of faith at once gave new significance to the individual person. If man by his own active faith has direct access to salvation then the Church ceases to be an indispensable instrument. The individual himself becomes the all-important centre. Luther's principle carries with it a shift from the objective aspect to the subjective, from conformity and submission to an immediate trust and confidence in God as Christ has revealed Him, " in which faith a man can die a thousand deaths." This protestant position was, or at least should have become, a proclamation of freedom and a declaration of the right of individual judg-

THE REFORMATION PERIOD

ment. Conscience, spiritual insight, becomes more important than the discovery of any external, infallible authority. If man himself and not a priestly ordination is what counts, then the distinction between clergy and laymen is merely one of function and not one of class or privilege. A man's spiritual life and power are determined by his faith, his insight, his character, and not by some magical act conferred upon him. So, too, the old artificial distinction between sacred and secular disappears. There are no special ways of being religious that are more sacred than any other ways so long as these ways are effective. The real test is life, deed, spirit —faithfulness, in short, in one's daily life and in one's sphere and calling. "What you do in your house," Luther once said, " is worth as much as if you did it up in heaven for our Lord God." And again : " It looks like a great thing when a monk renounces everything and goes into a cloister. It looks like a small thing when a woman works and scrubs and cleans in her house. But such work is a divine service far superior to the holiness and asceticism of monks and nuns."

This, and much more, is involved in Luther's *live idea*. Unfortunately the great reformer did not consistently carry it out ; did not set it at the very heart of all his work of reformation. It was courageously expounded only in those thrilling early years. I do not mean to say, or to imply, that at a certain date Luther changed character and became an altogether different man, quite unlike the hero of his early period. But it is an unmistakable fact that, when he saw the social and economic consequences of his reforming principles, when he realised that others—the liberty-loving peasants and the radical reformers—were inclined to push his principle farther than he intended to go with it, he vigorously called a halt and became a conservative, sometimes a reactionary, influence. He was, beyond question, jealous of his leadership, and when he saw any person, Carlstadt, for instance, or Zwingli, rising to a place of rival leadership, Luther unconsciously took a more extreme opposing position than he would have done if only the problem of doctrine or practice had been involved. All his later controversies sent him farther and farther in the direction of safety, authority and restraint, and inclined him to a course which tended to make the Reformation static and unprogressive.

In matters of doctrine Luther was always conservative and backward-looking. If only " doctrine " had been the issue in the Reformation period Luther need hardly have been called a " heretic." He was more extreme than most Roman Catholic contemporaries were in his maintenance of the dogma of original sin. He went all the way with St. Augustine, and a little farther, in declaring that man's will is wholly *unfree*. " The human will," he says, " is like a beast of burden. If God mounts it, it wishes and goes as God wills ; if Satan mounts it, it wishes and goes as Satan wills. *Nor can it choose its rider, nor*

THE REFORMATION PERIOD

betake itself to him it would prefer, but it is the riders who contend for its possession."[1] Man is impotent to *choose* his own salvation. He contributes nothing towards it—everything is done by divine Grace. The entire Augustinian system of divine Grace and human depravity is reinstated. The new feature is the fresh interpretation of faith and the recognition that the individual is in direct relation with God without the necessary intervention of the Church.

Luther, however, came very near to bringing back just that indispensable feature of the Church in the matter of sacraments. In his early writings, particularly the one on *The Babylonish Captivity of the Church*, he had shocked Erasmus by his attack on the sacramental system; but in his later controversies with the more liberal reformers, notably Zwingli, he swung over toward the old sacramental position, insisting that Grace is supernaturally conferred through baptism and the eucharist, so that a sacrament still is an *opus operatum*, a magical gift of Grace. He goes so far as to say: " External things in religion must precede internal experiences which come through external things, for God has resolved to give nobody the internal gifts except through the external things. He will give nobody the Spirit and faith without the use of external word and sign."[2]

In principle, Luther set men free from tradition and authority. He exalted individual conscience and

---
[1] *De servo arbitrio.* The Bondage of the Will. [Italics are mine.]
[2] *Wider die himmlischen Propheten vom Sacrament*, II.

personal insight. He started out to inaugurate a Church composed of those who had faith and spiritual vision, and who revealed an ability and power to proclaim the Word of God. But, in reality, he left in full operation a large relic of the ancient creeds, an extensive " rump " of superstition, tradition and magic, and a heavy inheritance of external authority. The result was that the new Church set itself up once more as the guardian of orthodoxy and proceeded, as the old Church had always done, to impose its views, its infallibilities, its indispensable functions, and to treat all dissidents and non-conformists as " heretics." [1]

The Calvinistic branch of the Reformed Church was still more strongly entrenched in the conceptions of authority and infallibility, more keen, too, in its scent for " heresy." Calvin felt it to be his mission to create an organisation and to formulate a theological system which could successfully compete with the Roman Catholic Church, and his system became the most impressive visible contribution of the Reformation. It gave the world the Huguenots of France, the Puritans of the English Commonwealth and of New England, Presbyterian Scotland, Reformed Switzerland, the Free Netherlands, and much besides.

There is no question of Calvin's gifts and genius.

[1] The best recent studies of Luther are Harnack's *Hist. of Dog.*, Vol. VII.; T. M. Lindsay's *Luther;* A. C. McGiffert's *Martin Luther, The Man and his Work;* Preserved Smith's *Life and Letters of Martin Luther;* Böhmer's *Luther;* and T. M. Lindsay's *A History of the Reformation.*

THE REFORMATION PERIOD

He belongs in the list of the greatest religious leaders in Christian history. He was born at Noyon, in Picardy, in 1509, became one of the foremost scholars of his age, fled to Switzerland to save his life, wrote the *Institutes of the Christian Religion* (first edition, Basle, 1536), went to Geneva in 1536, made it a model Christian city-state, and died there in 1564.

Calvin made less than Luther did of the sacraments. They are thought of only as external signs or symbols of inward spiritual realities. Calvin, however, far more than Luther, founded his entire Christian system on the Bible as the infallible Word of God. This he held to be God's one communication to the race. It contains, he believed, all revealed truth for all ages. All man ever needs to know in spiritual matters is in it, and without this Book these truths, found in it, could never have been discovered. It is the guide-book for daily life, the Magna Charta for all sound human legislation. Calvin's ideal state is to be a divinely-governed state, literally a theocracy. All the details of its life and activities are divinely revealed in the Word of God, and all the moral and social discipline of the city was vested exclusively in the consistory of ministers and elders, who were to act as delegates of the divine Sovereign.

Once more, as was the case with Luther, Calvin did not seriously alter the great body of doctrine which had been inherited from the historic Church. He shifted the stress and emphasis, but he preserved

THE CHURCH'S DEBT TO HERETICS

the central items of belief. He was more systematic and logical than Luther, but, like the latter, he was a guardian of St. Augustine's formulation of the faith. He was a great evangelical. He held emphatically to the ruin of man through the " fall." He accepted, and freshly emphasised, the unfree will, the gift of faith by divine Grace, the fact of election, the propitiatory sacrifice of Christ, salvation through faith in that sacrifice, the historic doctrine of the Trinity and the supernatural features of everything which concerns revelation and salvation. On what he believed to be a Scriptural basis, Calvin changed the organisation of the Church from an episcopal system to a system of presbyters, but he reduced in no particular the august and authoritative character of the Church. In fact, he widened its scope and conceived for it an unparalleled dignity and power as the vicar and representative of the Sovereign of the universe. This attitude attained its full meaning in the Puritan groups of England and America.

Once more, too, and even more emphatically than in the Lutheran communions, the Church which Calvin organised became the defender of " the faith once delivered," the guardian of orthodoxy. This Church, wherever it came into place and influence, was sensitively conscious of its infallibility and its unique authority. It was intolerant, and it believed rightly so, of all variations in doctrine and of all practices that seemed out of accord with its view of Scripture. It, therefore, had its large harvest of

THE REFORMATION PERIOD

" heretics " and its long list of persecutions. It must be said, however, that no other branch of the Reformation has so profoundly influenced modern history, or has made such an immense contribution. It quickly became the dominant form of protestant Christianity, and it has shaped many of the greatest currents of human life and thought. It brought men face to face with dread realities. It made God and His inscrutable sovereign will seem more real than earth or sky, and the one business of a man's life was to make his calling and election sure. Its members became stern fighters for their faith and their ideals. They would allow no earthly tyranny, and they would let no man in Church or State control human destiny.[1]

Besides these two great reforming movements led by Luther and Calvin, and the important Swiss Reformation led by Ulrich Zwingli, there were many other attempts made to effect a Reformation. Some of them were extremely radical movements, and aimed to bring about serious reconstruction, both of the Church and of the existing order of society. The economic and social factors which were involved in the Reformation were far greater than has been generally recognised, but all modern students of that epoch are now fully aware that there were many deeply-lying springs and motives in operation besides the distinctively religious ones, and among

[1] Williston Walker's *John Calvin, the Organizer of Reformed Protestantism*, is an excellent modern study of Calvin.

THE CHURCH'S DEBT TO HERETICS

these the desire for larger social and economic freedom was foremost. The dumb masses had reached about the limit of their silent endurance and they were beginning to find leadership and an articulate voice.

The Anabaptist movement, which represented the extreme left wing of the Reformation, was the expression of the common man's desire for a reformation that should radically reconstruct the world, and not merely lop off a few objectionable excrescences. They spoke for toilers and peasants; they felt the tragedy of the submerged classes; they were the champions of a new Church and a new world. They inherited the accumulated aims and aspirations of many lines and strains of heresy which I have already reviewed. The fact that they emerged at many widely separated points in Europe almost simultaneously, and had everywhere a similar programme, indicates a common background and a definite preparation. The translation of the New Testament, and the fresh propagation of its message and its ideals, did much to awaken a new hope in them and to create a vivid expectation, while Luther's early clarion call fired them with immense fervour.

The earliest leaders of the movement were young Swiss scholars and priests, who had an intense religious life and deep human sympathies. The most important persons in this early group were Conrad Grebel, Felix Mantz, William Roublin, Simon Stumpf and Ludwig Hetzer. They had been pro-

THE REFORMATION PERIOD

foundly stirred by their study of the mission of the Hebrew prophets and the message of the Gospels, and they believed that the time was now ripe for a revival of apostolic Christianity. They were also influenced by the "new prophets" of Zwickau, Münzer and Carlstadt, who powerfully voiced the hopes of the common people. The primary purpose which animated these young Swiss leaders was the construction of a Church entirely on the model of the New Testament, a Church which should be in every particular a copy of the apostolic pattern. If that aim was to be carried out, then, they believed, it must be first of all composed only of *believers*, a community of spiritual persons, possessed of faith and partakers of religious experience. The weakness of the old Church had been its vast number of merely nominal members, admitted at birth, but quite devoid of positive spiritual qualifications. To meet this situation they proposed to do away entirely with birthright membership and to have only members who were admitted on profession of personal faith. The baptism of infants seemed to them unwarranted, since, as they held, baptism can be *effective* only when taken as an act of personal faith, which no child is capable of, and as a sign and symbol of a new spiritual life.[1] To them baptism was important only as a feature of that New Testament Christianity

[1] The term Anabaptism means "rebaptism," and was given to the movement because its adherents "rebaptised" their members as adults; though they themselves maintained that it was not "rebaptism," since there can be no genuine baptism where faith is absent.

which they were reviving. They cared far more for the inward aspects of religion than they did for its outward practices.

Besides these essential points in their programme they held also that the Church must be kept " pure " by constantly winnowing out and excluding from membership those who fail to live and practise the Christian life. There must be a sharp distinction between the Church and the world, and those who are to compose the former must not adopt or accept the standards of the latter. For this reason they severed the Church and State completely. There was to be no entangling alliance between the two. The State must have no direct authority in the sphere of religion. Magistrates have no right to punish men for their faith or doctrine. Individual conscience in its relation with God must be absolutely free and untrammelled. They further endeavoured to remove the distinction between clergy and laity by insisting that all Christians, both men and women, have the same fundamental rights and privileges. There was to be no *hierarchy*, but only a fellowship of believers working together for common spiritual ends. They continued many of the peculiar scruples of the heretical sects, such as opposition to war, to the taking of life even in self-defence, and to the use of oaths, and they maintained also a very strict and rigorous standard of moral life for all Christians.

Two noble leaders of a similar movement appeared in Germany at about the same time that the Swiss

THE REFORMATION PERIOD

Anabaptists were inaugurating their programme. These men were Balthasar Hübmaier (born near Augsburg, 1480) and Hans Denck (born in Bavaria about 1495). They were both humanist scholars, pure-minded, noble-spirited, and both brave sufferers for their faith. Hübmaier was burned at the stake in Vienna, and Denck was brought to an early death by the persecutions which he suffered. They quickly had an immense following, and it looked for a time as though the whole world would become Anabaptist. Suddenly the uprising of the German peasants—an uprising which Münzer joined and inspired, though against the solemn advice of the Anabaptist leaders—gave the ruling class and the nobles a vivid sense of the danger to be expected from the new ideas and the new aspirations. Luther took the sternest possible attitude against the peasants, and declared that all who died fighting against them were " true martyrs before God." Münzer went to his death on the other side, the side which Luther damned as " venomous, pernicious and devilish."

The Anabaptists were non-resistant and were opposed to this outbreak, but they suffered immensely from the effect which it made upon the public mind. They were known to have radical-social views, and they were the purveyors of religious ideas that seemed to all existent churches revolutionary. A furious campaign of propaganda was set under way against Anabaptists everywhere, something like that

THE CHURCH'S DEBT TO HERETICS

which we have seen levelled against the Bolshevik revolution in our day. The word became a name of opprobrium, and all the forces of Government and Church were organised to hunt down the leaders of it and to exterminate them as pests. As the persecution swept down upon the sincere and honest Anabaptists with an almost unparalleled fury, and quenched their aspirations with fire or prison, it drove some of the new leaders into wildness and fanaticism. A popular movement, especially when it is radical and revolutionary, always attracts persons of unstable equilibrium, who are likely to damage the cause by hysteria, lack of balance and lack of restraint. So it happened now. The new leaders left the sphere of practical reform and resorted to apocalyptic hopes and expectations. Melchior Hoffmann, of Strasbourg, a fervid literalist, turned to the Apocalypse instead of the Gospels for his message, and aroused his eager hearers to look for a new world by miracle, a miracle which could be hastened by human action. Two of his Dutch disciples, Jan Matthys and Jan Bockelson, pushed literalism and fanaticism to their wildest extremes, and by the fierce spectacle of the Münster Kingdom gave the world some real ground for its horror of Anabaptism. Other forms of the movement tried with some success the experiment of a communistic society, modelled after the New Testament account in Acts iv. 32–37. Anabaptism was never a single, coherent, clearly organised movement. It lacked

THE REFORMATION PERIOD

fixed form, settled authority and corporate wisdom. It was always at the mercy and caprice of its local leaders and the conditions which happened to prevail when and where it emerged. The entire movement suffered terribly from the blunders of a few, and, as usual, the world accepted hostile propaganda as though it were truth.

Nevertheless, in spite of proscription, prison, blood and fire, the ideas at the heart of the movement spread with the power of contagion. They took strong root in Holland, England, the Tyrol, Bohemia and Poland. Many of their ideas caught hold and lived on even where no Anabaptist organisation existed, and out of the seed-truths, which no forces of Church or State could annihilate, there sprang, in the course of time, many important religious bodies—Baptist Societies and Mennonites. Many social and spiritual results followed, not the least of which is the basic and fundamental position of religion in relation to government in the United States, the general respect for the rights of conscience, and the prevailing recognition that religion is a matter to be settled between the individual soul and God. These free privileges were purchased at a great cost—the lives of more than thirty thousand martyrs—and they are now enjoyed by multitudes who have no consciousness that those who first proclaimed the ideals died for them.

No less important were the aims and ideals which were championed by much smaller contemporary

THE CHURCH'S DEBT TO HERETICS

groups of men who are often called "Spiritual Reformers." They have frequently been merged in one chaotic mass with the Anabaptists and have been closely identified with them. Some of them did begin their mission in fellowship with the Anabaptist groups, but they soon differentiated themselves from that movement, as notably Hans Denck did, and dedicated themselves to a different task and a different goal. These men had come more powerfully under the influence of Erasmus than most of the Anabaptists had done. They shared his enthusiasm for the Gospel ideals of the Kingdom of God, and they shared in a still stronger degree his abhorrence of theology. They were all readers and lovers of the mystics, and they were themselves mystically-minded. The inner life, the Light and Spirit of God revealed in the human soul, seemed to them the supreme reality for religion, and they turned their thoughts away from the problems and tasks of building a visible Church to the more important task, as they believed, of constructing the invisible Church— "the blessed community" of the Spirit.

Sebastian Franck, of Donauwörth (born 1499), was the most articulate interpreter of their ideals, but Hans Denck, Johann Bünderlin, a disciple of Denck, and Christian Entfelder are beautiful and saintly exponents of the same gospel. Caspar Schwenckfeld, a scholar, a reformer, a preacher of righteousness, a voluminous writer, the exponent of "the middle way," and the founder of the Schwenck-

THE REFORMATION PERIOD

feldians, belongs also in this list. In the same list belongs also the brilliant and interesting French scholar, who was a keen and trenchant critic and opponent of Calvin, Sebastian Castellio (1515–63). Mention should be made in this connection of the Spaniard, Juan de Valdès, the Dutch reformer, Dirck Coornhert, and the English liberal preacher, John Everard. Jacob Boehme (1575–1624), the Silesian mystic and constantly persecuted heretic, gathered up and gave voluminous, though not always lucid, expression to the type of Christianity which these spiritual reformers longed to see replace the theological and ecclesiastical types. Boehme was a powerful opponent of Lutheran doctrines, insisting upon an inward and vital transformation of life through the direct work of the Divine Spirit as the one condition of salvation.

One more branch of the Reformation—also a left wing movement—must be briefly considered, that which usually goes under the name of Socinianism, though its exponents are sometimes called " Romantic Reformers." It was an attempt to think Christianity through to its foundations and to re-interpret it freshly, sincerely and boldly without regard to tradition or dogma, but with an awakened and kindled passion for ethical and social ideals. There were many brave and adventurous spirits in Italy, at the birth of the Reformation, who were eager to take part in the new era of life and thought and to join in the great adventure of rebuilding the Christian structure. Michael Servetus (1511–53), a Spanish physician, an early defender of the circulation of the blood, was their forerunner in this field. He was a strong opponent of the doctrine of the Trinity [*De Trinitatis Erroribus* (1531), *Dialogues on the Trinity* (1532)]. He revived an adoptionist interpretation of Christ, who was, he taught, Man by nature but Son of God by grace and Divine gift. Servetus was burned at the stake in Geneva at the instigation of Calvin in 1553. It was in reference to this act that Castellio wrote to Calvin the memorable words: " To burn a man is not to defend a doctrine, *it is to burn a man!*" Lelio Sozini (1525–62), a scholar, a mystic, like his friend, Camillo of Sicily, a man of high moral quality, laid the foundations of the Socinian movement, though, either because he was cautious or, as is more likely, because he had not thought the problems through at the time of his early death, he left his ideas in unpublished notes. These ideas were brought to mature development and put into a system of thought by his nephew, Fausto Sozzini (the latter always spelling his name with two z's). Fausto (1539–64) was born in Sienna. He was a sound, well-trained scholar. In 1578 he issued his radical treatise, *De Jesu Christo servatore*. It professes to develop and defend the position of his uncle, Lelio, and it was a sweeping attack upon the theological position of the evangelical reformers. The book resulted in securing for Sozzini an invitation to Poland, where he developed and expounded

THE REFORMATION PERIOD

his doctrine, and where, in spite of popular attacks, he had a safe retreat and won many followers. He directed the anti-Trinitarian movement in Transylvania as well as in Poland, though he never joined the anti-Trinitarian Church in Poland, on account of his view that the ceremony of baptism was unnecessary, the spiritual condition of heart and life being the only important matter. He did not call himself a Unitarian, though the word was used unofficially by the Socinians and was officially used as early as 1600. It was formally adopted in 1638. He felt his mission in life to be the presentation of a religion of life in terms to meet the needs of his age. He wanted to purge Christianity of all superstition and of those supernatural factors that had been introduced into it in unscientific and unphilosophical ages, and to set it forth in its intrinsic power. He was a gentle soul, simple in spirit, humble in mind, honest, fearless, an absolute pacifist and believer in the sufficiency of moral and spiritual forces. He took a very modern view of the Scriptures and a very lofty view of Christ, though not the orthodox one. It is an interesting historical fact that he exerted an important influence upon the distinguished Dutch scholar, Hugo Grotius.[1]

This liberal, rationalising effort provoked tre-

---

[1] The best modern treatment of the Socinian movement is a series of articles by Alexander Gordon in the *Theological Review* for 1879 on "The Sozzini and their School." The best source of the early movement is F. Trechsel's *Die Protestantischen Antitrinitarier*, etc. (1844).

mendous opposition, those who led it and those who accepted it were fiercely maligned and anathematised, but it had a large following, and it helped to produce the modern temper of mind, the desire to eliminate the mediæval accumulations of theology and to return to a religion of life and spirit. The extensive books of Sozzini do not give the outlook, the atmosphere, or the spiritual quality of Christianity as our best modern day interpreters present it. He was rationalistic and too much involved in the theological battles of his period to suit us to-day, but he was bravely endeavouring, as were the Spiritual Reformers and the Anabaptists, to rediscover Christ's Christianity, and to set it forth in its simplicity and power without the accretions of the centuries.

CHAPTER X

MODERN HERESIES AND HERETICS

THE Reformation stands as one of the greatest watersheds in history. Every current of life and thought takes a new direction after that epoch. The ancient barriers were passed. The shackles and restraints on human thought were broken. The magic of tradition, authority and dogma was over. In one sense heresy ends here. The Reformation stands, in principle at least, for freedom of search for truth. The methods of research, however, were at this stage inadequate. Sound canons of criticism were still wanting. It long remained easier to dogmatise than to discover and verify *truth*, but the foundation for the modern world was at last laid. The great point was established that the dead hand of the past should no longer control human thought; truth was fearlessly to be pursued and found and held. And, in so far as that idea prevailed, *heresy* became synonymous with *error*—not error in the old sense of non-conformity to an established standard, but rather error in the sense of failure to fit the facts and laws of the eternal nature of things.

But, in spite of the fact that the watershed was crossed at the Reformation and a new era had begun, the outlook and mental habits of the past were by no means entirely left behind. The well-known air of infallibility long survived in the new age. Dogmatic assertion was still a familiar method, and suspicions and charges of heresy remained short and easy ways of dealing with unwelcome opponents ; and ways, too, that entailed grave dangers and perils to the heretic. The heresies of the new era, however, can be briefly and concisely dealt with, for we are concerned here mainly with the direction of the forward march toward ends of life and truth.

The most important step towards a broader and more liberal theology, after the Reformation period, was that taken by the Dutch scholar and popular preacher, Jacobus Arminius (1560–1609). From the point of view of established Calvinism, Arminius was a daring heretic, but, historically, he belongs in the small list of the very greatest contributors to liberal and rational theology. He was not a " radical" like Pelagius or Sozzini, but rather a balanced, synthesising and harmonising thinker, finding a middle position between naturalism on the one hand and fatalism on the other. Arminius built upon the moral consciousness in man and was a powerful interpreter of the ethical relations between God and man. He protested against the extreme Calvinistic theory —the supralapsarian theory—of predestination. God's work in relation to man's salvation is wholly moral and spiritual ; never capricious. God foresaw man's sin but He did not decree it. Arminius further laid great emphasis on the human factor in salvation. Man is always a moral agent in the pro-

MODERN HERESIES AND HERETICS

cess of redemption; never a fatalistic "instrument" for irresistible Grace. He insisted on free will and held firmly to the view that man is responsible for his own destiny through acts of faith or of unbelief. He denied that Adam's sin was imputed to the human race; sin to be sin must be an act of personal choice. The work of Grace and truth is always moral and persuasive. Grace is not a compelling force. It is revealed in the gentle, tender appeal of the Holy Spirit, to which man may say either yes or no, and the answer of the soul is big with destiny. The Arminian position has been the prevailing tendency of Anglican theology—a tendency which showed itself in England before Arminius formulated it. It is strongly in evidence in the "Latitudemen" of the seventeenth century, and it reached its culmination in the evangelicalism of the Wesleys in the eighteenth century. John Wesley was a great Arminian prophet.

Another line of heretical tendency culminated in another English prophet, George Fox (1624–91), the founder of the Quakers. Many spiritual and reforming movements were confluent and preparatory to the movement which he organised and guided. The most important of these preparatory movements was that of the "Seekers," who emerged from the earlier groups of "Spiritual Reformers." They owed their specific origin to Dirck Coornhert (born 1522), a Dutch spiritual reformer, whose teaching first brought Arminius to his epoch-making position. His disciples were called "Collegiants"

THE CHURCH'S DEBT TO HERETICS

in Holland, and " Seekers," or " Waiters," in England. They exalted the Light of Christ in the soul, omitted the sacraments, had no ordained ministers, met for worship in silence, and spoke or prayed only as they felt moved by the Spirit. Another powerful stream of influence toward the Quaker movement came from Jacob Boehme, the Silesian mystic, already mentioned. He set forth a profound conception of salvation as an inward process wrought in the human soul by the immediate presence and activity of the living Christ. He was persecuted as a heretic by the local Lutheran authorities, but his writings had a far-reaching influence, and still remain quick and vitalising. His greatest direct English disciple was William Law (1686–1761). " The Family of Love " ; the best elements of the sect nicknamed the " Ranters " ; those who were mystically inclined among the English Anabaptists, and the disciples of spiritual leaders like John Everard, John Saltmarsh and William Dell, helped to swell the early Quaker ranks. The definite inspiration and the organising leadership came from George Fox. He revolted as a youth from the Calvinistic theology which he heard preached in the Anglican church of his birthplace, Fenny Drayton, and for four years he wandered about seeking for a religion of reality and vitality. Through a series of profound inward experiences Fox felt himself, in 1647, commissioned to preach and expound a very simple type of religion which he believed to be apostolic Christianity revived. It met with a quick response from those

MODERN HERESIES AND HERETICS

who were prepared for the message and he soon had a large following. He suffered fierce persecution, and his followers both in England and America were harried vigorously until something like toleration was established by the English Revolution of 1688.

The Quakers stood for a Christianity of inward life and experience, largely freed from dogma, ritual and ecclesiasticism. They were mystics in type and disposition. They discounted outward performances and claimed that the realities of religion must be inwardly experienced. They greatly exalted the worth and possibilities of human life. They stood for the spiritual equality of the sexes. They championed the cause of the less fortunate classes and races of men. They, like St. Francis, had immeasurable faith in the reconciling and transforming power of love, and they went about the world practising human love and joyfully bearing the burdens of human suffering.

Their form of worship was extremely simple and completely congregational. They tried the experiment of having no ordained ministers, of considering all believers priests unto God, and of assuming that the Spirit of God would guide and direct the Church and initiate and inspire the appropriate messages for the hour. They insisted that revelation is continuous, and that God is the spiritual life and inner environment of all seeking and obedient souls. Quaker history is the story of this experiment. This attempt to exhibit a religion of experience and

THE CHURCH'S DEBT TO HERETICS

demonstration, this faith in the present Christ as an inward revealing power, this conviction that love will work as a way of life, have been extremely effective, and it is an attitude and temper of mind which admirably fits the modern Christian spirit.

Within the Roman Catholic communion there broke forth in the seventeenth century a wave of quietistic Mysticism. It concentrated upon a type of contemplation, or " prayer of quiet," by which, in a single act of faith, it was believed that inexhaustible Grace was infused into the soul and a state of spiritual fecundity attained. The Church condemned as heretical the three greatest leaders of this extraordinary movement: Molinos, Fénelon and Madame Guyon ; but, though treated with disapproval at its source, the essential traits of Quietism were taken up in many Protestant centres, and its influence as a spiritual force became widespread during the eighteenth century.

The outstanding characteristic tendency of the eighteenth century was an excessive confidence in Rationalism and a corresponding distrust of feelings, emotions and enthusiasm. The tendency was far too general to be treated as a heresy, since it appears alike both within and outside the circles of orthodoxy, but it was, at any rate, the prolific mother of heresies. Deism was one of its specific offshoots. This was an attempt to reduce Christianity to a sheer naturalism. It accepted God as a first cause, an abstract Supreme Being, but it eliminated from our world miracle, inspiration, everything that could

MODERN HERESIES AND HERETICS

be called the supernatural, and it considered the sphere of the divine to be wholly beyond the region of nature. It reached its culmination in the writings of Voltaire, Thomas Paine, and the French encyclopædists, but it was a widespread popular view in England, in France, and in colonial America. The orthodox opponents of it were themselves rationalistic and semi-deistic, and they were, for the most part, lacking in spiritual depth, and they were hampered by their failure to find a sound historical and critical basis of approach to the fundamental issues. Out of the welter there eventually emerged a number of great constructive movements which have shaped our modern world. The earliest of these movements, and the most intense one, was the evangelical revival led by the Wesleys and Whitefield. This was in no proper sense heretical, though it offended conventional ecclesiastical taste and judgment, was subjected to mob violence and led to the organisation of new non-conformist bodies. It awakened a lethargic world to fresh spiritual fervour, it intensified religious experience, and it produced a great revival of philanthropy and humanitarian spirit.

Another immense contribution was the birth of critical philosophy, the foundations of which were laid by Kant (1724–1804). This movement, often treated as heretical by official orthodoxy, has been the profoundest philosophical influence during the last hundred years. It permeated the greatest creations of literature during that century, and it is still a vital and shaping intellectual force. Coleridge,

THE CHURCH'S DEBT TO HERETICS

Wordsworth, Goethe, Carlyle and Emerson are the most illuminating literary interpreters of it, and, through them, it has infused itself as a spirit and temper into the lives of multitudes who have never read Kant or his successors. In this same general period modern Unitarianism and organised Universalism had their birth as a revolt and protest against extreme forms of theological dogmatism. John Biddle (1615–62) is the "father" of modern Unitarianism, but Joseph Priestley and James Martineau in England, and Jonathan Mayhew and William Ellery Channing in America were pillar interpreters of the movement. It began in revolt and vigorous protest. It aroused an almost unbelievable tide of theological hate. It invaded many communions. It produced divisions in homes and in churches. The old debates are dull, sad reading. There was narrowness on both sides and failure to apprehend the deeper central truths which underlay both wings. But there can now be no doubt that the Unitarian protest has helped in the end to bring a truer conception of God and man, a broader Christian spirit, a more liberal theology, a larger humanitarianism, and a sounder Biblical scholarship. Universalism, too, was a protest against extremes of doctrine which shocked the fundamental sentiments of the awakened human soul. It was an ancient protest, as old, in fact, as Christian theology itself. But it was brought to a new and organised form by John Murray (1741–1815), and later by Hosea Ballou, who was born in New Hampshire in 1771.

MODERN HERESIES AND HERETICS

The movement was, in its popular forms, often crude and unethical, but its clearest interpreters were possessed with a deep moral passion and were honest, fearless champions of the righteousness and grace of God as revealed in Christ, and they have helped in some measure to bring a sounder view of sin and its inherent consequences, and a truer and more moral view of the life beyond as a realm of genuine ethical and spiritual issues.

There have been few modern changes in religious thought so important and significant as the gradual change from forensic conceptions of salvation to vital, moral and spiritual conceptions of it. In one case salvation was thought of as an external transaction; in the other case it is thought of as an inward process. Jacob Boehme, George Fox and William Law were champions of this vital process, and they were counted to be heretics for their spiritual insight. Thomas Erskine of Linlathen, Macleod Campbell, Charles Kingsley, Frederick Denison Maurice and Frederick W. Robertson belong in the noble list of interpreters of salvation as a vital process, and they felt and heralded a new meaning in the Cross of Christ. Horace Bushnell, of Connecticut, was, however, the most profound and effective interpreter of this vital and dynamic faith. They were all criticised, judged and condemned by the old theologians for their deviation, but they helped to make a freer world of thought and a more spiritual Christianity, and they gave a new sense of reality to the Incarnation. Phillips Brooks was the most inspired preacher of the new message, and John Greenleaf Whittier was the most persuasive poetic interpreter of it.

Meantime the battle lines of religious thought began to be drawn up at a range and on a scale unparalleled in history, the final issues of which are still unsettled. The irresistible march of science and historical criticism is one of the most amazing features of the modern world. It has introduced a new basis of authority, and it has fundamentally altered the interpretation of man's origin and destiny. The doctrine of evolution has more profoundly affected religious conceptions than has any other single scientific theory during the entire range of human history, though the Copernican theory is a close second to it.

It seemed at first to many that Christianity could not survive if evolution and the conclusions of higher criticism were admitted to be valid. Here was a " heresy " with which no truce could be made ! But slowly the deeper wisdom of the spiritual group has asserted itself. In the long run *truth*, wherever found, proves to be of God, and it reveals itself as a constructive, not a destructive, force. The fact that the universe has been an unfolding process, that life is a developing affair, that revelation has been conformed to temporal and historical situations, is a support to a spiritual faith, not a hindrance to it. That man has come up out of earlier and lower forms of life to his present stage, and is big with potency of yet larger life, fits in with a spiritual order

MODERN HERESIES AND HERETICS

rather than with a material one. On the whole the new and revolutionary views make for and support a more fundamentally spiritual religion than did the intellectual theories of a hundred years ago.

The real issue, after all, is the issue between a spiritual interpretation of the universe and a naturalistic, materialistic one. The outstanding heresy of our time is materialism, a theory of the universe which eliminates significance, values, purpose, freedom, personal initiative, the reality of the soul, the transcendence of Spirit, man's communion and fellowship with a Great Companion. Not less deadly and disastrous is that practical materialism—that moral heresy—which makes money and the "things" money buys the measure of life, and which regards success and pleasure as the real ends and goals of life.

But these crude, half-truth theories are doomed to wane and pass as the fuller, irresistibly-breaking light of truth climbs higher in the sky. To alter slightly Emerson's line: Half-gods go when Gods arrive. The more we know about the universe the more certain is it that at bottom it is Spirit. The more we know about man the more certain is it that he is fundamentally spiritual, *i.e.*, akin to Spirit, and the more we know about history—cosmic or human—the more certain it becomes that the whole affair is *dramatic*, and prophetic of a moral, spiritual and purposeful *dénouement*.

I have given no account of the agony and heartbreak which underlie every step of spiritual advance.

THE CHURCH'S DEBT TO HERETICS

> " Never on custom's oiléd grooves
> The world to a higher level moves,
> But grates and grinds with friction hard
> On granite boulder and flinty shard.
> The heart must bleed before it feels,
> The pool be troubled before it heals."

The lonely prophet of a larger truth must, in any age, suffer as Jeremiah did. He is bound to be misunderstood and attacked. He must expect to be scorned and vilified by those whom he disturbs. Truth is very precious and very *costly*. It is only those who are ready to pay the price for it that can be its disciples and torch-bearers. But when they are sincere, patient, enduring, humble, reverent, brave and allied with God, they do, in His own time, carry the precious standard forward. Such persons may well say with Browning's " Paracelsus " :

> " I go to prove my soul!
> I see my way as birds their trackless way.
> I shall arrive ! what time, what circuit first,
> I ask not : but unless God send His hail
> Or blinding fire-balls, sleet or stifling snow,
> In some time, His good time, I shall arrive :
> He guides me and the bird."

INDEX

Abelard, Peter, 185–196, 202
Adoptionists, 70–75, 174, 177
Albertus Magnus, 216
Albigenses, 179, 183
Albigensian Crusade, 209, 210
Alogi, 68–69
Anabaptists, 202, 232–237, 242, 246
Apollinarius, 108–109, 113, 115
Apostles' Creed, 57–58
Arianism, 81, 85–103, 183
Aristotle, 22, 88 n., 109, 124, 216
Arius, 85–88, 92–95, 99–100, 110
Arminius, Jacobus, 244–245
Arnold of Brescia, 150, 190, 196–202
Athanasius, 90, 92–94, 96–97, 99, 101, 103, 120
Augustine, St., of Hippo, 45, 122, 123–125, 126–127, 128–130, 144, 161, 167–168, 169–170, 227, 230

Bernard, St., of Clairvaux, 145, 161, 190–191, 196, 199, 201, 203, 204
Bernard of Tours, 147
Boehme, Jacob, 239, 246, 251
Bogomils, 177–179, 183
Bonaventura, 157–158
Brooks, Phillips, 251
Bushnell, Horace, 251

Calvin, John, 228–231, 239, 240
Campbell, Macleod, 251
Canon of Scripture, 57, 143
Carlstadt, 226, 233
Cathari, 150, 179–183
Cerinthus, 38–41, 70
Channing, William Ellery, 250
Clement of Alexandria, 36, 81
Constantine, Emperor, 90, 94–95, 99, 107, 166
Councils,
    Constantinople (A.D. 381), 101
    Constantinople (A.D. 431), 130
    Constantinople (A.D. 553), 111 n.
    Ephesus (A.D. 431), 117
    Second Lateran (A.D. 1139), 198
    Third Lateran (A.D. 1179), 176
    Nicæa (A.D. 325), 80, 95–97
    Oxford (A.D. 1160), 176
    Rome (A.D. 430), 116
    Sens (A.D. 1140), 191, 196, 198
    Verona (A.D. 1184), 208

Creed,
    Apostles', 57–58
    Early, 77, 131
    Nicene, 95–97, 99, 101, 104, 120
Cyprian, 14
Cyril of Alexandria, 111, 112, 114–119, 121

Deism, 248–249
Dionysius, St., 144, 145, 188
Docetism, 41, 53–58
Donatists, 164–169, 207

Ebionites, 39, 71 n.
Eckhart, Meister, 218
Erasmus, 219–221, 227, 238
Erigena, John Scotus, 145–146, 148, 161
Erskine, Thomas, of Linlathen, 251
Eternal Gospel, The, 153–157
Eusebius of Cæsarea, 71–72, 95
Eusebius of Nicomedia, 86, 87, 97
Eutychianism, 118, 119

Family of Love, The, 246
Fox, George, 126, 202, 245–246, 251
Francis, St., of Assisi, 154, 197, 204, 247
Franciscans, 16, 154 ff., 210–212
Fraticelli, 159, 210, 212
Frederick Barbarossa, 150, 200
Friends of God, The, 217

Gnostics, 26, 28–60, 173, 177, 178
Gregory, St., the Great, 144
Gregory of Nazianzus, 101, 120
Gregory of Nyssa, 83, 101
Gregory VII., Pope, 184
Grotius, Hugo, 241

Heloise, 187, 189
Hilary of Poitiers, 99
Hippolytus, 36, 41, 68, 70, 71 n., 78
Huguenots, 228
Hus, John, 214, 217, 222

Ignatius, St., 56, 57, 59, 60, 163
Irenæus, St., 36, 38, 41, 63, 163

Jerome, St., 123, 129
Joachim da Fiori, 149–154, 161
Joan of Arc, 214
John, St., Chrysostom, 105–106, 111, 116, 124

INDEX

Julian, Emperor, 99, 100–101
Justin, 47, 63
Justinian, Emperor, 111 n., 143

KANT, Immanuel, 249–250
à Kempis, Thomas, 16, 219
Kingsley, Charles, 251

LAW, William, 246, 251
Lollards, 214
Lombard, Peter, 190
Luther, Martin, 48, 98, 219, 220, 221–228, 229, 230, 231, 235

MANI or Manichæus, 169, 171
Manichæan movement, 126, 130, 169–173, 174, 177, 178
Marcion, 41, 45–53
Marcionites, 172, 173, 174
Martineau, James, 250
Maurice, F. D., 251
Mennonites, 237
Minucius, Felix, 63
Mithras, 30
Modalism, 75–80, 138
Monarchianism, 69–70, 76, 88
Monophysitism, 118
Montanism, 135–144, 146
Montanus, 136, 161
de Montfort, Simon, 209
Münzer, Thomas, 233, 235
Mysticism, 144–145

NESTORIAN Church, 121–122
Nestorius, 111–122, 124, 130
Nicolaitans, 35–37

OLIVI, Peter John, 158, 210
Origen, 66, 81–83, 86, 108
Orphic Circles, 30

PATRIPASSIANS, 76–77, 78
Paul, St., 15, 17, 20, 29, 33–35, 45, 48, 58, 63, 110, 133, 162–163
Paul of Samosata, 73–75, 86, 108, 118, 173
Paulicians, 173–177, 183
Pelagians, 111, 122–130, 244
Peter the Venerable, 191–192, 202, 203
Petrobrusians, 202–203, 206
Philo, 28, 63, 64–65
Plato, 22, 32, 81, 88 n., 125
Plotinus, 22, 81, 132

Polycarp, St., 38, 46, 56, 163
Presbyterians, 228, 230
Priestley, Joseph, 250
Priscillian, 131
Puritans, 228, 230
Pythagorean brotherhoods, 30

QUAKERS, 245–248
Quietism, 248

RANTERS, 246
Robertson, F. W., 251

SABELLIANISM, 87, 97, 99
Sabellius, 78–80, 131
Salvation, 29, 42, 48-50, 61, 125–129, 192–195
Savonarola, Girolamo, 219
Schwenckfeld, Caspas, 238
Seekers, 245–246
Servetus, Michael, 240
Simonians, 37–38
Socinianism, 239–242
Sozzini, Fausto, 240–242, 244
Spiritual Franciscans, 155–161, 210–212
Spiritual Reformers, 238–239, 242, 245
Stoics, 22, 64, 125

TAULER, John, 218 n., 222
Tertullian, 36, 46, 48, 63, 66, 69, 76, 77, 140–142
Theodore of Mopsuestia, 105–111, 116, 121, 122, 124, 130

ULFILAS, Bishop, 102
Unitarianism, 89, 241, 250
Universalism, 250–251
University of Paris, 145, 146, 148, 210

VALENTINIANS, 41
Voltaire, 249

WALDENSES, 16, 201, 204–208, 211, 213
Waldo, Peter, 204–205
Wesley, John, 245, 249
Whitefield, George, 249
Whittier, John G., 252
William of Occam, 211
Wyclif, John, 201, 208, 212–214, 217, 222

ZWINGLI, Ulrich, 226, 227, 231

www.ingramcontent.com/pod-product-compliance
Lightning Source LLC
Chambersburg PA
CBHW070246230426
43664CB00014B/2419